# Be
# Inspired

DAMEYAN O. COLE

# DEDICATION

This book is dedicated to those who desire to make a positive contribution to the world. It is only those who think differently can do differently.

# CONTENTS

# QUOTE

"Attention is the key to life. Whatever you really give your attention to, you become. Whatever you really concentrate upon will come into your life. We grow into the thing that fills our thoughts as inevitably as the stream merges into the ocean at last."

— **Emmet Fox**

# MOTIVATION QUOTES

1. Tough times don't last. Tough people do. – **Robert H. Schuller**

2. It's not about perfect. It's about effort. – **Jillian Michaels**

3. If you want something you have never had, you must be willing to do something you have never done. – **Thomas Jefferson**

4. Never give up on a dream just because of the time it will take to accomplish it. The time will pass anyway. – **Earl Nightingale**

5. Everything you've ever wanted is on the other side of fear. – **George Addair**

6. If people are not laughing at your goals, your goals are too small. – **Azim Premji**

7. Work hard in silence, let your success be your noise. – **Frank Ocean**

8. If you want to live a happy life, tie it to a goal, not

to people or things. – **Albert Einstein**

9. If you are not willing to risk the usual you will have to settle for the ordinary. – **Jim Rohn**

10. Life begins at the end of your comfort zone. – **Neale Donald Walsch**

11. The greatest pleasure in life is doing what people say you cannot do. – **Walter Bagehot**

12. Hard work beats talent when talent doesn't work hard. – **Tim Notke**

13. An entire sea of water can't sink a ship unless it gets inside the ship. Similarly, the negativity of the world can't put you down unless you allow it to get inside you. – **Goi Nasu**

14. If you are depressed you are living in the past. If you are anxious you are living in the future. If you are at peace you are living in the present. – **Lao Tzu**

15. The first step to getting anywhere is deciding you're no longer willing to stay where you are. – **Anonymous**

16. Knowing is not enough, we must apply. Willing is not enough, we must do.– **Bruce Lee**

17. Doubt kills more dreams than failure ever will. – **Suzy Kassem**

18. I am not what happened to me, I am what I choose to become.– **Carl Gustav Jung**

19. Great minds discuss ideas. Average minds discuss events. Small minds discuss people. – **Eleanor Roosevelt**

20. A problem is a chance for you to do your best. – **Duke Ellington**

21. If it is important to you, you will find a way. If not, you'll find an excuse. – **Ryan Blair**

22. You don't have to be great to start, but you have to start to be great. – **Zig Ziglar**

23. The pain you feel today will be the strength you feel tomorrow. – **Unknown**

24. Don't wait for the right moment to start, start and make each moment right. – **Roy T. Bennett**

25. Life is 10% what happens to you and 90% how you react to it. – **Charles R. Swindoll**

26. Only I can change my life. No one can do it for me. – **Carol Burnett**

27. Start where you are. Use what you have. Do what

you can. – **Arthur Ashe**

28. Our greatest weakness lies in giving up. The most certain way to succeed is always to try just one more time. – **Thomas A. Edison**

29. Always believe that something wonderful is about to happen. – **Coco Chanel**

30. Difficult roads always lead to beautiful destinations. – **Zig Ziglar**

31. Look in the mirror. That's your competition. – **John Assaraf**

32. When you know what you want, and want it bad enough, you'll find a way to get it. – **Jim Rohn**

33. Two things define you: Your patience when you have nothing and your attitude when you have everything. – **Imam Ali**

34. A river cuts through rock, not because of its power, but because of its persistence. – **Jim Watkins**

35. Failure will never overtake me if my determination to succeed is strong enough. – **Og Mandino**

36. Beginning today, treat everyone you meet as if they were going to be dead by midnight. Extend to them all the care, kindness and understanding you

can muster, and do it with no thought of any reward. Your life will never be the same again. – **Og Mandino**

37. Do not wait; the time will never be 'just right.' Start where you stand, and work with whatever tools you may have at your command, and better tools will be found as you go along. – **George Herbert**

38. Believe in yourself! Have faith in your abilities! Without a humble but reasonable confidence in your own powers you cannot be successful or happy. – **Norman Vincent Peale**

39. Someday is not a day of the week. – **Denise Brennan–Nelson**

40. Infuse your life with action. Don't wait for it to happen. Make it happen. Make your own future. Make your own hope. Make your own love. And whatever your beliefs, honor your creator, not by passively waiting for grace to come down from upon high, but by doing what you can to make grace happen... yourself, right now, right down here on Earth. – **Bradley Whitford**

41. With the new day comes new strength and new thoughts. – **Eleanor Roosevelt**

42. You are not here merely to make a living. You are here in order to enable the world to live more

amply, with greater vision, with a finer spirit of hope and achievement. You are here to enrich the world, and you impoverish yourself if you forget the errand. – **Woodrow Wilson**

43. Keep your eyes on the stars, and your feet on the ground. – **Theodore Roosevelt**

44. Consult not your fears but your hopes and your dreams. Think not about your frustrations, but about your unfulfilled potential. Concern yourself not with what you tried and failed in, but with what it is still possible for you to do. – **Pope John XXIII**

45. Do the difficult things while they are easy and do the great things while they are small. A journey of a thousand miles must begin with a single step. – **Lao Tzu**

46. What you get by achieving your goals is not as important as what you become by achieving your goals. – **Zig Ziglar**

47. Set your goals high, and don't stop till you get there. – **Bo Jackson**

48. Your talent is God's gift to you. What you do with it is your gift back to God. – **Leo Buscaglia**

49. What you do today can improve all your

tomorrows. – **Ralph Marston**

50. Problems are not stop signs, they are guidelines. – **Robert H. Schuller**

51. Do the one thing you think you cannot do. Fail at it. Try again. Do better the second time. The only people who never tumble are those who never mount the high wire. This is your moment. Own it. – **Oprah Winfrey**

52. Learning is the beginning of wealth. Learning is the beginning of health. Learning is the beginning of spirituality. Searching and learning is where the miracle process all begins. – **Jim Rohn**

53. A creative man is motivated by the desire to achieve, not by the desire to beat others. – **Ayn Rand**

54. It always seems impossible until it's done. – **Nelson Mandela**

55. There is no passion to be found playing small – in settling for a life that is less than the one you are capable of living. – **Nelson Mandela**

56. Follow your dreams, work hard, practice and persevere. Make sure you eat a variety of foods, get plenty of exercise and maintain a healthy lifestyle. – **Sasha Cohen**

57. We are taught you must blame your father, your sisters, your brothers, the school, the teachers – but never blame yourself. It's never your fault. But it's always your fault, because if you wanted to change you're the one who has got to change. – **Katharine Hepburn**

58. Poverty was the greatest motivating factor in my life. – **Jimmy Dean**

59. When something is important enough, you do it even if the odds are not in your favor. – **Elon Musk**

60. I don't believe you have to be better than everybody else. I believe you have to be better than you ever thought you could be. – **Ken Venturi**

61. When you reach the end of your rope, tie a knot in it and hang on. – **Franklin D. Roosevelt**

62. Knowing is not enough; we must apply. Willing is not enough; we must do. – **Johann Wolfgang von Goethe**

63. Learn from the past, set vivid, detailed goals for the future, and live in the only moment of time over which you have any control: now. – **Denis Waitley**

64. Setting goals is the first step in turning the invisible into the visible. – **Tony Robbins**

65. You are never too old to set another goal or to dream a new dream. – **Les Brown**

66. If you want to succeed you should strike out on new paths, rather than travel the worn paths of accepted success. – **John D. Rockefeller**

67. There is only one corner of the universe you can be certain of improving, and that's your own self. – **Aldous Huxley**

68. By failing to prepare, you are preparing to fail. – **Benjamin Franklin**

69. Be miserable. Or motivate yourself. Whatever has to be done, it's always your choice. – **Wayne Dyer**

70. Where there is a will, there is a way. If there is a chance in a million that you can do something, anything, to keep what you want from ending, do it. Pry the door open or, if need be, wedge your foot in that door and keep it open. – **Pauline Kael**

71. If you want to conquer fear, don't sit home and think about it. Go out and get busy. – **Dale Carnegie**

72. If you're going through hell, keep going. –

**Winston Churchill**

73. In order to succeed, we must first believe that we can. – **Nikos Kazantzakis**

74. Set your sights high, the higher the better. Expect the most wonderful things to happen, not in the future but right now. Realize that nothing is too good. Allow absolutely nothing to hamper you or hold you up in any way. – **Eileen Caddy**

75. I really believe that everyone has a talent, ability, or skill that he can mine to support himself and to succeed in life. – **Dean Koontz**

76. You simply have to put one foot in front of the other and keep going. Put blinders on and plow right ahead. – **George Lucas**

77. I learned that we can do anything, but we can't do everything... at least not at the same time. So think of your priorities not in terms of what activities you do, but when you do them. Timing is everything. – **Dan Millman**

78. The way to get started is to quit talking and begin doing. – **Walt Disney**

79. Get action. Seize the moment. Man was never intended to become an oyster. – **Theodore Roosevelt**

80. The first step toward success is taken when you refuse to be a captive of the environment in which you first find yourself. – **Mark Caine**

81. Determine never to be idle. No person will have occasion to complain of the want of time who never loses any. It is wonderful how much may be done if we are always doing. – **Thomas Jefferson**

82. You can't build a reputation on what you are going to do. – **Henry Ford**

83. If you don't design your own life plan, chances are you'll fall into someone else's plan. And guess what they have planned for you? Not much. – **Jim Rohn**

84. Decide what you want, decide what you are willing to exchange for it. Establish your priorities and go to work. – **H. L. Hunt**

85. You must take action now that will move you towards your goals. Develop a sense of urgency in your life. – **H. Jackson Brown, Jr.**

86. Either I will find a way, or I will make one. – **Philip Sidney**

87. The hardships that I encountered in the past will help me succeed in the future. – **Philip Emeagwali**

88. Always continue the climb. It is possible for you to do whatever you choose, if you first get to know who you are and are willing to work with a power that is greater than ourselves to do it. – **Ella Wheeler Wilcox**

89. Never, never, never give up. – **Winston Churchill**

90. Whatever you want in life, other people are going to want it too. Believe in yourself enough to accept the idea that you have an equal right to it. – **Diane Sawyer**

91. Press forward. Do not stop, do not linger in your journey, but strive for the mark set before you. – **George Whitefield**

92. If you don't like how things are, change it! You're not a tree. – **Jim Rohn**

93. Perseverance is failing 19 times and succeeding the 20th. – **Julie Andrews**

94. Arriving at one goal is the starting point to another. – **John Dewey**

95. You just can't beat the person who never gives up. – **Babe Ruth**

96. You will never win if you never begin. – **Helen**

**Rowland**

97. Even if you fall on your face, you're still moving forward. – **Victor Kiam**

98. One way to keep momentum going is to have constantly greater goals. – **Michael Korda**

99. If you think you can do it, you can. – **John Burroughs**

100. Set yourself earnestly to see what you are made to do, and then set yourself earnestly to do it. – **Phillips Brooks**

# SUCCESS QUOTES

1.  The only place where success comes before work is in the dictionary. – **Vidal Sassoon**

2.  I never dreamed about success, I worked for it. – **Estee Lauder**

3.  If you focus on success, you'll have stress. But if you pursue excellence, success will be guaranteed. – **Deepak Chopra**

4.  Success is nothing more than a few simple disciplines, practiced every day. – **Jim Rohn**

5.  Seven Steps to Success 1) Make a commitment to grow daily. 2) Value the process more than events. 3) Don't wait for inspiration. 4) Be willing to sacrifice pleasure for opportunity. 5) Dream big. 6) Plan your priorities. 7) Give up to go up. – **John C. Maxwell**

6.  I never did anything worth doing by accident, nor did any of my inventions come indirectly through accident, except the phonograph. No, when I have fully decided that a result is worth getting, I go

about it, and make trial after trial, until it comes. – **Thomas Edison**

7.  Successful people have libraries. The rest have big screen TVs. – **Jim Rohn**

8.  The foundation stones for a balanced success are honesty, character, integrity, faith, love and loyalty. – **Zig Ziglar**

9.  Action is the foundational key to all success. – **Pablo Picasso**

10. Don't be distracted by criticism. Remember the only taste of success some people get is to take a bite out of you. – **Zig Ziglar**

11. It is not where you start but how high you aim that matters for success. – **Nelson Mandela**

12. The way of success is the way of continuous pursuit of knowledge. – **Napoleon Hill**

13. Success is doing ordinary things extraordinarily well. – **Jim Rohn**

14. . The secret of success is to do the common thing uncommonly well. – **John D. Rockefeller Jr**.

15. The secret to success is to know something nobody else knows. – **Aristotle Onassis**

16. Do not judge me by my successes, judge me by how many times I fell down and got back up again. – **Nelson Mandela**

17. Successful people don't have fewer problems. They have determined that nothing will stop them from going forward. – **Ben Carson**

18. The difference between a successful person and others is not a lack of strength, not a lack of knowledge, but rather a lack in will. – **Vince Lombardi**

19. If you start today to do the right thing, you are already a success even if it doesn't show yet. – **John C. Maxwell**

20. Success usually comes to those who are too busy to be looking for it. – **Henry David Thoreau**

21. Many of life's failures are people who did not realize how close they were to success when they gave up. – **Thomas A. Edison**

22. You know you are on the road to success if you would do your job, and not be paid for it. – **Oprah Winfrey**

23. I'm always asked, 'What's the secret to success?' But there are no secrets. Be humble. Be hungry.

And always be the hardest worker in the room. – **Dwayne Johnson**

24. The successful warrior is the average man, with laser– like focus. – **Bruce Lee**

25. There are no secrets to success: don't waste time looking for them. Success is the result of perfection, hard work, learning from failure, loyalty to those for whom you work, and persistence. – **Colin Powell**

26. Whenever you see a successful business, someone once made a courageous decision. – **Peter F. Drucker'**

27. Success seems to be connected with action. Successful people keep moving. They make mistakes, but they don't quit. – **Conrad Hilton**

28. It is better to fail in originality than to succeed in imitation. – **Herman Melville**

29. Don't be afraid to give up the good to go for the great. – **John D. Rockefeller**

30. I find that the harder I work, the more luck I seem to have. – **Thomas Jefferson**

31. There are two types of people who will tell you that you cannot make a difference in this world:

those who are afraid to try and those who are afraid you will succeed. – **Ray Goforth**

32. Keep on going, and the chances are that you will stumble on something, perhaps when you are least expecting it. I never heard of anyone ever stumbling on something sitting down. – **Charles F. Kettering**

33. As long as you keep going, you'll keep getting better. And as you get better, you gain more confidence. That alone is success. – **Tamara Taylor**

34. A successful man is one who can lay a firm foundation with the bricks that other throw at him. – **David Brinkley**

35. Education is the key to success in life, and teachers make a lasting impact in the lives of their students. – **Solomon Ortiz**

36. If you can dream it, you can do it. – **Walt Disney**

37. Success is not the key to happiness. Happiness is the key to success. If you love what you are doing, you will be successful. – **Albert Schweitzer**

38. . Would you like me to give you a formula for success? It's quite simple, really: Double your rate of failure. You are thinking of failure as the enemy

of success. But it isn't at all. You can be discouraged by failure or you can learn from it, so go ahead and make mistakes. Make all you can. Because remember that's where you will find success. – **Thomas J. Watson**

39. Success is no accident. It is hard work, perseverance, learning, studying, sacrifice and most of all, love of what you are doing or learning to do. – **Pele**

40. Without continual growth and progress, such words as improvement, achievement, and success have no meaning. – **Benjamin Franklin**

41. Success isn't always about greatness. It's about consistency. Consistent hard work leads to success. Greatness will come.– **Dwayne Johnson**

42. The price of success is hard work, dedication to the job at hand, and the determination that whether we win or lose, we have applied the best of ourselves to the task at hand.– **Vince Lombardi**

43. Take up one idea. Make that one idea your life – think of it, dream of it, live on that idea. Let the brain, muscles, nerves, every part of your body, be full of that idea, and just leave every other idea alone. This is the way to success. – **Swami Vivekananda**

44. Your success and happiness lies in you. Resolve to keep happy, and your joy and you shall form an invincible host against difficulties. – **Helen Keller**

45. At the end of the day, you are solely responsible for your success and your failure. And the sooner you realize that, you accept that, and integrate that into your work ethic, you will start being successful. As long as you blame others for the reason you aren't where you want to be, you will always be a failure. – **Erin Cummings**

46. Success isn't measured by money or power or social rank. Success is measured by your discipline and inner peace. – **Mike Ditka**

47. The path from dreams to success does exist. May you have the vision to find it, the courage to get on to it, and the perseverance to follow it. – **Kalpana Chawla**

48. Your success depends mainly upon what you think of yourself and whether you believe in yourself. – **William J. H. Boetcker**

49. The key to success is to be honest, follow your passion and not someone else's path.– **Urvashi Rautela**

50. Success has always been easy to measure. It is the distance between one's origins and one's final

achievement. – **Michael Korda**

51. If you create incredible value and information for others that can change their lives – and you always stay focused on that service – the financial success will follow. – **Brendon Burchard**

52. No man can be a failure if he thinks he's a success; If he thinks he is a winner, then he is. – **Robert W. Service**

53. Success is not in what you have, but who you are. – **Bo Bennett**

54. Self– knowledge is the foundation of real success. – **Rachel Simmons**

55. The first thing successful people do is view failure as a positive signal to success. – **Brendon Burchard**

56. The path to success is to take massive, determined action. **Tony Robbins**

57. You don't have to be a genius or a visionary or even a college graduate to be successful. You just need a framework and a dream. – **Michael Dell**

58. There's more to life than success, and if you can try to be more well– rounded, you'll be able to enjoy your success more. It won't own you or control

you. – **Ricky Williams**

59. The relationships we have with people are extremely important to success on and off the job. – **Zig Ziglar**

60. The single most important key to success is to be a good listener. – **Kelly Wearstler**

61. The foundation stones for a balanced success are honesty, character, integrity, faith, love and loyalty. – **Zig Ziglar**

62. Focused, hard work is the real key to success. Keep your eyes on the goal, and just keep taking the next step towards completing it. If you aren't sure which way to do something, do it both ways and see which works better. – **John Carmack**

63. A little more persistence, a little more effort, and what seemed hopeless failure may turn to glorious success. – **Elbert Hubbard**

64. One important key to success is self– confidence. An important key to self– confidence is preparation. – **Arthur Ashe**

65. Obstacles are necessary for success because in selling, as in all careers of importance, victory comes only after many struggles and countless defeats. – **Og Mandino**

66. For success, attitude is equally as important as ability. – **Walter Scott**

67. Success comes to those who dedicate everything to their passion in life. To be successful, it is also very important to be humble and never let fame or money travel to your head. – **A. R. Rahman**

68. The level of our success is limited only by our imagination and no act of kindness, however small, is ever wasted. – **Aesop**

69. The foundation of success in life is good health: that is the substratum fortune; it is also the basis of happiness. A person cannot accumulate a fortune very well when he is sick. – **P. T. Barnum**

70. For me, money is not my definition of success. Inspiring people is a definition of success. – **Kanye West**

71. At the end of the day, the most overwhelming key to a child's success is the positive involvement of parents. – **Jane D. Hull**

72. You were designed for accomplishment, engineered for success, and endowed with the seeds of greatness. – **Zig Ziglar**

73. Success doesn't necessarily come from

breakthrough innovation but from flawless execution. A great strategy alone won't win a game or a battle; the win comes from basic blocking and tackling. – **Naveen Jain**

74. Think twice before you speak, because your words and influence will plant the seed of either success or failure in the mind of another. – **Napoleon Hill**

75. Honesty and loyalty are key. If two people can be honest with each other about everything, that's probably the biggest key to success. – **Taylor Lautner**

76. It doesn't matter whether you are pursuing success in business, sports, the arts, or life in general: The bridge between wishing and accomplishing is discipline. – **Harvey Mackay**

77. Success is like a wild horse. If you do not know how to handle it, it will throw you off and look for another rider who can handle it well. – **Ajith Kumar**

78. I do not think that there is any other quality so essential to success of any kind as the quality of perseverance. It overcomes almost everything, even nature. – **John D. Rockefeller**

79. Honesty and integrity are absolutely essential for success in life – all areas of life. The really good

news is that anyone can develop both honesty and integrity. – **Zig Ziglar**

80. Don't wait to be successful at some future point. Have a successful relationship with the present moment and be fully present in whatever you are doing. That is success. – **Eckhart Tolle**

81. Humility is the true key to success. Successful people lose their way at times. They often embrace and overindulge from the fruits of success. Humility halts this arrogance and self– indulging trap. Humble people share the credit and wealth, remaining focused and hungry to continue the journey of success. – **Rick Pitino**

82. You know you've reached true success the day you become truly humble. That's the day you stop needing to prove to the world – and yourself – that you've accomplished something meaningful. – **Naveen Jain**

83. 'No one can make you successful; the will to success comes from within.' I've made this my motto. I've internalized it to the point of understanding that the success of my actions and/or endeavors doesn't depend on anyone else, and that includes a possible failure.– **Fabrizio Moreira**

84. No one succeeds without effort... Those who

succeed owe their success to perseverance. – **Ramana Maharshi**

85. The first step toward success is taken when you refuse to be a captive of the environment in which you first find yourself. – **Mark Caine**

86. Our goals can only be reached through a vehicle of a plan, in which we must fervently believe, and upon which we must vigorously act. There is no other route to success. – **Pablo Picasso**

87. Perseverance is a great element of success. If you only knock long enough and loud enough at the gate, you are sure to wake up somebody. **Henry – Wadsworth Longfellow**

88. The secret to success is good leadership, and good leadership is all about making the lives of your team members or workers better. – **Tony Dungy**

89. Most people give up just when they're about to achieve success. They quit on the one yard line. They give up at the last minute of the game one foot from a winning touchdown. – **Ross Perot**

90. Success is not a destination, but the road that you're on. Being successful means that you're working hard and walking your walk every day. You can only live your dream by working hard towards it. That's living your dream. – **Marlon**

**Wayans**

91. Success is peace of mind which is a direct result of self– satisfaction in knowing you did your best to become the best you are capable of becoming. – **John Wooden**

92. Just remember, you can't climb the ladder of success with your hands in your pockets. – **Arnold Schwarzenegger**

93. Success is almost totally dependent upon drive and persistence. The extra energy required to make another effort or try another approach is the secret of winning. – **Denis Waitley**

94. Patience, persistence and perspiration make an unbeatable combination for success. – **Napoleon Hill**

95. Success is not measured by what you accomplish, but by the opposition you have encountered, and the courage with which you have maintained the struggle against overwhelming odds. – **Orison Swett Marden**

96. There's a lot of blood, sweat, and guts between dreams and success. – **Bear Bryant**

97. It's good to test yourself and develop your talents and ambitions as fully as you can and achieve

greater success; but I think success is the feeling you get from a job well done, and the key thing is to do the work. – **Peter Thiel**

98. Success is not the absence of failure; it's the persistence through failure. – **Aisha Tyler**

99. There is never just one thing that leads to success for anyone. I feel it always a combination of passion, dedication, hard work, and being in the right place at the right time. – **Lauren Conrad**

100. I will form good habits and become their slave. And how will I accomplish this difficult feat? Through these scrolls it will be done, for each scroll contains a principle which will drive a bad habit from my life and replace it with one which will bring me closer to success. – **Og Mandino**

# INSPIRATION QUOTES

1. Nothing will work unless you do. – **Maya Angelou**

2. The best and most beautiful things in the world cannot be seen or even touched – they must be felt with the heart. **Helen Keller**

3. I have learned over the years that when one's mind is made up, this diminishes fear. – **Rosa Parks**

4. I will love the light for it shows me the way, yet I will endure the darkness because it shows me the stars. – **Og Mandino**

5. Change your thoughts and you change your world. – **Norman Vincent Peale**

6. If You Are Working On Something That You Really Care About, You Don't Have To Be Pushed. The Vision Pulls You. – **Steve Jobs**

7. Whether you think you can or think you can't, you're right. – **Henry Ford**

8. Perfection is not attainable, but if we chase perfection we can catch excellence. – **Vince Lombardi**

9. When everything seems to be going against you, remember that the airplane takes off against the wind, not with it. – **Henry Ford**

10. The most common way people give up their power is by thinking they don't have any. – **Alice Walker**

11. Your work is going to fill a large part of your life, and the only way to be truly satisfied is to do what you believe is great work. And the only way to do great work is to love what you do. If you haven't found it yet, keep looking. Don't settle. As with all matters of the heart, you'll know when you find it. – **Steve Jobs**

12. The only limit to our realization of tomorrow will be our doubts of today. – **Franklin D. Roosevelt**

13. Develop an 'attitude of gratitude'. Say thank you to everyone you meet for everything they do for you. – **Brian Tracy**

14. If you always put limit on everything you do, physical or anything else. It will spread into your work and into your life. There are no limits. There are only plateaus, and you must not stay there, you must go beyond them. – **Bruce Lee**

15. The best preparation for tomorrow is doing your best today. – **H. Jackson Brown, Jr.**

16. People who are crazy enough to think they can change the world, are the ones who do. – **Rob Siltane**

17. We may encounter many defeats but we must not be defeated. – **Maya Angelou**

18. Failure will never overtake me if my determination to succeed is strong enough. – **Og Mandino**

19. Attitude is a choice. Happiness is a choice. Optimism is a choice. Kindness is a choice. Giving is a choice. Respect is a choice. Whatever choice you make makes you. Choose wisely. – **Roy T. Bennett**

20. Always do your best. What you plant now, you will harvest later. – **Og Mandino**

21. The two most important days in your life are the day you are born and the day you find out why. – **Mark Twain**

22. My mission in life is not merely to survive, but to thrive; and to do so with some passion, some compassion, some humor, and some style. – **Maya Angelou**

23. Today a reader, tomorrow a leader. – **Margaret Fuller**

24. If you love life, don't waste time, for time is what life is made up of. – **Bruce Lee**

25. Pain is inevitable. Suffering is optional. – **Haruki Murakami**

26. Don't let yesterday take up too much of today. – **Will Rogers**

27. You learn more from failure than from success. don't let it stop you. Failure builds character. – **Unknown**

28. I've learned that people will forget what you said, people will forget what you did, but people will never forget how you made them feel. – **Maya Angelou**

29. I can't change the direction of the wind, but I can adjust my sails to always reach my destination. – **Jimmy Dean**

30. Build your own dreams, or someone else will hire you to build theirs. – **Farrah Gray**

31. Don't wish it were easier. Wish you were better. – **Jim Rohn**

32. Live as if you were to die tomorrow. Learn as if you were to live forever. – **Mahatma Gandhi**

33. I hated every minute of training, but I said, Don't quit. Suffer now and live the rest of your life as a champion. – **Muhammad Ali**

34. The greatest pleasure in life is doing what people say you cannot do. – **Walter Bageh**

35. It's Not Whether You Get Knocked Down, It's Whether You Get Up. – **Vince Lombardiot**

36. If you don't know where you are going, you will probably end up somewhere else. – **Laurence J. Peter**

37. The Man Who Has Confidence In Himself Gains The Confidence Of Others. – **Hasidic Proverb**

38. Happiness is not something you postpone for the future; it is something you design for the present. – **Jim Rohn**

39. Try not to become a man of success. Rather become a man of value. – **Albert Einstein**

40. Let us sacrifice our today so that our children can have a better tomorrow. – **A. P. J. Abdul Kalam**

41. First they ignore you, then they ridicule you, then they fight you, and then you win. – **Mahatma Gandhi**

42. Discipline is the bridge between goals and accomplishment. – **Jim Rohn**

43. Life is too short to waste your time on people who don't respect, appreciate, and value you. – **Roy Bennett**

44. Whatever the mind of man can conceive and believe, it can achieve. – **Napoleon Hill**

45. If you want to lift yourself up, lift up someone else. – **Booker T. Washington**

46. The real opportunity for success lies within the person and not in the job. – **Zig Ziglar**

47. Intelligence is the ability to adapt to change. – **Stephen Hawking**

48. Courage is the most important of all the virtues because without courage, you can't practice any other virtue consistently. — **Maya Angelou**

49. The pessimist sees difficulty in every opportunity. the optimist sees opportunity in every difficulty. – **Winston Churchill**

50. Take responsibility of your own happiness, never put it in other people's hands. — **Roy T. Bennett**

51. When you get into a tight place and everything goes against you, till it seems as though you could not hang on a minute longer, never give up then, for that is just the place and time that the tide will turn. – **Harriet Beecher Stowe**

52. We generate fears while we sit. We overcome them by action. – **Dr. Henry Link**

53. Security is mostly a superstition. Life is either a daring adventure or nothing. – **Helen Keller**

54. What you lack in talent can be made up with desire, hustle and giving 110% all the time. – **Don Zimmer**

55. Start by doing what's necessary; then do what's possible; and suddenly you are doing the impossible. – **Francis of Assisi**

56. Don't judge each day by the harvest you reap but by the seeds that you plant. – **Robert Louis Stevenson**

57. Keep your face always toward the sunshine – and shadows will fall behind you. – **Walt Whitman**

58. I believe there's an inner power that makes winners

or losers. And the winners are the ones who really listen to the truth of their hearts. – **Sylvester Stallone**

59. Once I knew only darkness and stillness... my life was without past or future... but a little word from the fingers of another fell into my hand that clutched at emptiness, and my heart leaped to the rapture of living. – **Helen Keller**

60. I have not failed. I've just found 10,000 ways that won't work. – **Thomas A. Edison**

61. Teamwork is the ability to work together toward a common vision, the ability to direct individual accomplishments toward organizational objectives. It is the fuel that allows common people to attain uncommon results. – **Andrew Carnegie**

62. When we love, we always strive to become better than we are. When we strive to become better than we are, everything around us becomes better too. – **Paulo Coelho, The Alchemist**

63. Hold fast to dreams, For if dreams die. Life is a broken– winged bird, That cannot fly. — **Langston Hughes**

64. The flower that blooms in adversity is the rarest and most beautiful of all. — **Walt Disney Company, Mulan**

65. Respect other people's feelings. It might mean nothing to you, but it could mean everything to them. — **Roy T. Bennett**

66. You need to learn how to select your thoughts just the same way you select your clothes every day. This is a power you can cultivate. If you want to control things in your life so bad, work on the mind. That's the only thing you should be trying to control. — **Elizabeth Gilbert**

67. Do you want to know who you are? Don't ask. Act! Action will delineate and define you. — **Thomas Jefferson**

68. We delight in the beauty of the butterfly, but rarely admit the changes it has gone through to achieve that beauty. — **Maya Angelou**

69. What you do makes a difference, and you have to decide what kind of difference you want to make. – **Jane Goodall**

70. It's only after you've stepped outside your comfort zone that you begin to change, grow, and transform. — **Roy T. Bennett**

71. There is no royal road to anything. One thing at a time, all things in succession. That which grows fast, withers as rapidly. That which grows slowly,

endures. – **Josiah Gilbert Holland**

72. Be not afraid of life. Believe that life is worth living, and your belief will help create the fact. – **William James**

73. Even if you're on the right track, you'll get run over if you just sit there. – **Will Rogers**

74. Courage is the first of human qualities because it is the quality which guarantees all others. – **Winston Churchill**

75. Every truth passes through three stages before it is recognized. In the first, it is ridiculed. In the second, it is opposed. In the third, it is regarded as self evident. – **Arthur Schopenhauer**

76. Our character is not defined in the good times, but in the hard times. – **Paul Brodie**

77. If you want something out of life you have to go out there and get it, because it is not just going to be given to you. – **Kelvin Waites**

78. Having a specific meaning and purpose in your life helps to encourage you towards living a fulfilling and inspired life. – **Vic Johnson**

79. Don't waste your time in anger, regrets, worries, and grudges. Life is too short to be unhappy. – **Roy**

**T. Bennett**

80. Nothing is impossible, the word itself says I'm possible! – **Audrey Hepburn**

81. If you look at what you have in life, you'll always have more. If you look at what you don't have in life, you'll never have enough. – **Oprah Winfrey**

82. Believe you can and you're halfway there. – **Theodore Roosevelt**

83. To handle yourself, use your head; to handle others, use your heart. – **Eleanor Roosevelt**

84. Too many of us are not living our dreams because we are living our fears. – Les Brown

85. Alone, we can do so little; together we can do so much. – **Helen Keller**

86. Twenty years from now you will be more disappointed by the things that you didn't do than by the ones you did do, so throw off the bowlines, sail away from safe harbor, catch the trade winds in your sails. Explore, Dream, Discover. – **Mark Twain**

87. I've missed more than 9000 shots in my career. I've lost almost 300 games. 26 times I've been trusted to take the game winning shot and missed.

I've failed over and over and over again in my life. And that is why I succeed. – **Michael Jordan**

88. I am not a product of my circumstances. I am a product of my decisions. – **Stephen Covey**

89. The most difficult thing is the decision to act, the rest is merely tenacity. – **Amelia Earhart**

90. The meaning of life is to find your gift. The purpose of life is to give it away. – **Anonymous**

91. If you are free, you need to free somebody else. If you have some power, then your job is to empower somebody else. – **Toni Morrison**

92. If you are not willing to risk the unusual, you will have to settle for the ordinary**. – Jim Rohn**

93. Learn to say 'no' to the good so you can say 'yes' to the best. – **John C. Maxwell**

94. If you want something you never had, you have to do something you've never done. – **Thomas Jefferson**

95. Understand: you are one of a kind. Your character traits are a kind of chemical mix that will never be repeated in history. There are ideas unique to you, a specific rhythm and perspective that are your strengths, not your weaknesses. You must not be

afraid of your uniqueness. – **Robert Greene**

96. The easiest way to change the world is to change yourself. – **Maxime Lagacé**

97. The secret of getting ahead is getting started. – **Mark Twain**

98. A ship is always safe a shore but that is not what it's built for. – **Albert Einstein**

99. Shoot for the moon and if you miss you will still be among the stars. – **Les Brown**

100. If you can dream it, then you can achieve it. You will get all you want in life if you help enough other people get what they want. – **Zig Ziglar**

# LEADERSHIP QUOTES

1. Management is doing things right; leadership is doing the right things. – **Peter F. Drucker**

2. Men make history and not the other way around. In periods where there is no leadership, society stands still. Progress occurs when courageous, skillful leaders seize the opportunity to change things for the better. – **Harry S Truman**

3. The world needs new leadership, but the new leadership is about working together. – **Jack Ma**

4. No man will make a great leader who wants to do it all himself or get all the credit for doing it. – **Andrew Carnegie**

5. Leadership to me means duty, honor, country. It means character, and it means listening from time to time. – **George W. Bush**

6. Leadership is a way of thinking, a way of acting and, most importantly, a way of communicating. – **Simon Sinek**

7. Before you are a leader, success is all about growing yourself. When you become a leader, success is all about growing others. – **Jack Welch**

8. You don't have to hold a position in order to be a leader. – **Henry Ford**

9. Leadership is not about titles, positions or flowcharts. It is about one life influencing another. – **John C. Maxwell**

10. Ninety percent of leadership is the ability to communicate something people want. – **Dianne Feinstein**

11. Outstanding leaders go out of their way to boost the self– esteem of their personnel. If people believe in themselves, it's amazing what they can accomplish. – **Sam Walton**

12. Leadership is not about a title or a designation. It's about impact, influence and inspiration. Impact involves getting results, influence is about spreading the passion you have for your work, and you have to inspire team– mates and customers. – **Robin S. Sharma**

13. The key to successful leadership is influence, not authority. – **Kenneth H. Blanchard**

14. Leadership is about vision and responsibility, not

power. – **Seth Berkley**

15. He who cannot be a good follower cannot be a good leader. – **Aristotle**

16. Optimism is the ultimate definition of a leader. A leader has to look optimistically at what is ahead while not ignoring the challenges that must be overcome. Those challenges are in government, politics, world leadership, and even in community life. – **Linda McMahon**

17. A leader is one who knows the way, goes the way, and shows the way. – **John C. Maxwell**

18. The greatest leader is not necessarily the one who does the greatest things. He is the one that gets the people to do the greatest things. – **Ronald Reagan**

19. When the leader lacks confidence, the followers lack commitment. – **John C. Maxwell**

20. Management is about arranging and telling. Leadership is about nurturing and enhancing. – **Tom Peters**

21. If your actions create a legacy that inspires others to dream more, learn more, do more and become more, then, you are an excellent leader. – **Dolly Parton**

22. Good leadership consists of showing average people how to do the work of superior people. – **John D. Rockefeller**

23. One of the most important things for any leader is to never let anyone else define who you are. And you define who you are. I never think of myself as being a woman CEO of this company. I think of myself as a steward of a great institution. – **Ginni Rometty**

24. Leaders are made, they are not born. They are made by hard effort, which is the price which all of us must pay to achieve any goal that is worthwhile. – **Vince Lombardi**

25. Ultimately, leadership is not about glorious crowning acts. It's about keeping your team focused on a goal and motivated to do their best to achieve it, especially when the stakes are high and the consequences really matter. It is about laying the groundwork for others' success, and then standing back and letting them shine. – **Chris Hadfield**

26. A person, who no matter how desperate the situation, gives others hope, is a true leader. – **Daisaku Ikeda**

27. I think one of the keys to leadership is recognizing that everybody has gifts and talents. A good leader

will learn how to harness those gifts toward the same goal. **– Ben Carson**

28. A person who is quietly confident makes the best leader. **– Fred Wilson**

29. The task of the leader is to get people from where they are to where they have not been. **– Henry Kissinger**

30. The test of leadership is not to put greatness into humanity, but to elicit it, for the greatness is already there. **– James Buchanan**

31. A leader takes people where they want to go. A great leader takes people where they don't necessarily want to go, but ought to be. **– Rosalynn Carter**

32. A leader does not deserve the name unless he is willing occasionally to stand alone. **– Henry Kissinger**

33. The secret to success is good leadership, and good leadership is all about making the lives of your team members or workers better. **– Tony Dungy**

34. You learn far more from negative leadership than from positive leadership. Because you learn how not to do it. And, therefore, you learn how to do it. **– Norman Schwarzkopf**

35. To be a leader, you have to make people want to follow you, and nobody wants to follow someone who doesn't know where he is going. – **Joe Namath**

36. Leadership is something you earn, something you're chosen for. You can't come in yelling, 'I'm your leader!' If it happens, it's because the other guys respect you. – **Ben Roethlisberger**

37. The greatest leader is not necessarily the one who does the greatest things. He is the one that gets the people to do the greatest things. – **Ronald Reagan**

38. I believe in servant leadership, and the servant always asks, 'Where am I needed most?' – **Mike Pence**

39. Leaders are made, they are not born. They are made by hard effort, which is the price which all of us must pay to achieve any goal that is worthwhile. – **Vince Lombardi**

40. Positive leadership – conveying the idea that there is always a way forward – is so important, because that is what you are here for – to figure out how to move the organization forward. Critical to doing that is reinforcing the idea that everyone is included. – **Alan Mulally**

41. Leadership is about making the right decision and the best decision before, sometimes, it becomes entirely popular. – **Martin O'Malley**

42. Leaders must be close enough to relate to others, but far enough ahead to motivate them. – **John C. Maxwell**

43. For success of any mission, it is necessary to have creative leadership. Creative leadership is vital for government, non– governmental organisations as well as for industries. – **A. P. J. Abdul Kalam**

44. I think leadership is more than just being able to cross the t's and dot the i's. It's about character and integrity and work ethic. – **Steve Largent**

45. To me, leadership is about encouraging people. It's about stimulating them. It's about enabling them to achieve what they can achieve – and to do that with a purpose. – **Christine Lagarde**

46. Leadership is a matter of having people look at you and gain confidence, seeing how you react. If you're in control, they're in control. – **Tom Landry**

47. A leader is best when people barely know he exists, when his work is done, his aim fulfilled, they will say: we did it ourselves. – **Lao Tzu**

48. There is no greater name for a leader than mother

or father. There is no leadership more important than parenthood. – **Sheri L. Dew**

49. One of the tests of leadership is the ability to recognize a problem before it becomes an emergency. – **Arnold H. Glasow**

50. A successful person finds the right place for himself. But a successful leader finds the right place for others. – **John C. Maxwell**

51. Leadership is the challenge to be something more than average**. – Jim Rohn**

52. As we look ahead into the next century, leaders will be those who empower others. – **Bill Gates**

53. Leadership is not a basket of tricks or strategies or skills that you pull out. Leadership begins with the quality of the person. – **Frances Hesselbein**

54. Whether you empower one person or the free world, that is leadership. – **Julie Foudy**

55. The day the soldiers stop bringing you their problems is the day you stopped leading them. They have either lost confidence that you can help them or concluded that you do not care. Either case is a failure of leadership. – **Colin Powell**

56. Becoming a leader is synonymous with becoming

yourself. It is precisely that simple and it is also that difficult. – **Warren Bennis**

57. Leadership is a potent combination of strategy and character. But if you must be without one, be without the strategy. –**Norman Schwarzkopf**

58. The challenge of leadership is to be strong, but not rude; be kind, but not weak; be bold, but not a bully; be thoughtful, but not lazy; be humble, but not timid; be proud, but not arrogant; have humor, but without folly. – **Jim Rohn**

59. Leadership is a privilege to better the lives of others. It is not an opportunity to satisfy personal greed. – **Mwai Kibaki**

60. The supreme quality for leadership is unquestionably integrity. Without it, no real success is possible, no matter whether it is on a section gang, a football field, in an army, or in an office. – **Dwight D. Eisenhower**

61. At the heart of great leadership is a curious mind, heart, and spirit. – **Chip Conley**

62. The greatest gift of leadership is a boss who wants you to be successful. – **Jon Taffer**

63. It is better to lead from behind and to put others in front, especially when you celebrate victory when

nice things occur. You take the front line when there is danger. Then people will appreciate your leadership. – **Nelson Mandela**

64. Leadership is having a compelling vision, a comprehensive plan, relentless implementation, and talented people working together. – **Alan Mulally**

65. I know of no single formula for success. But over the years I have observed that some attributes of leadership are universal and are often about finding ways of encouraging people to combine their efforts, their talents, their insights, their enthusiasm and their inspiration to work together.– **Queen Elizabeth II**

66. Leadership contains certain elements of good management, but it requires that you inspire, that you build durable trust. For an organization to be not just good but to win, leadership means evoking participation larger than the job description, commitment deeper than any job contract's wording. – **Stanley A. McChrystal**

67. It is better to have a lion at the head of an army of sheep, than a sheep at the head of an army of lions. – **Daniel Defoe**

68. Effective leadership is putting first things first. Effective management is discipline, carrying it out.

**Stephen Covey**

69. True leadership lies in guiding others to success. In ensuring that everyone is performing at their best, doing the work they are pledged to do and doing it well. – **Bill Owens**

70. There are good leaders who actively guide and bad leaders who actively misguide. Hence, leadership is about persuasion, presentation and people skills. – **Shiv Khera**

71. When the best leader's work is done the people say, 'We did it ourselves.' – **Lao Tzu**

72. A true leader has the confidence to stand alone, the courage to make tough decisions, and the compassion to listen to the needs of others. He does not set out to be a leader, but becomes one by the equality of his actions and the integrity of his intent. – **Douglas MacArthur**

73. One of my beliefs about leadership is it's not how many followers you have, but how many people you have with different opinions that you can bring together and try to be a good listener. – **Robert Kraft**

74. One of the topics I'm most passionate about is servant leadership – the greatest leaders recognize that they're here to serve, not to be served. – **Ken**

**Blanchard**

75. I suppose leadership at one time meant muscles; but today it means getting along with people. – **Mahatma Gandhi**

76. Without initiative, leaders are simply workers in leadership positions. – **Bo Bennett**

77. Leadership is getting someone to do what they don't want to do, to achieve what they want to achieve. – **Tom Landry**

78. Leadership is an opportunity to serve. It is not a trumpet call to self – importance. – **J. Donald Walters**

79. I forgot to shake hands and be friendly. It was an important lesson about leadership. – **Lee Iacocca**

80. In order to cultivate a set of leaders with legitimacy in the eyes of the citizenry, it is necessary that the path to leadership be visibly open to talented and qualified individuals of every race and ethnicity. – **Sandra Day O'Connor**

81. Leadership is an active role; 'lead' is a verb. But the leader who tries to do it all is headed for burnout, and in a powerful hurry. – **Bill Owens**

82. Leadership is about doing the right thing, even if it

going against a vast number of naysayers and mediocre people. – **N. R. Narayana Murthy**

83. What you do has far greater impact than what you say. – **Stephen Covey**

84. Innovation distinguishes between a leader and a follower. – **Steve Jobs**

85. True leadership stems from individuality that is honestly and sometimes imperfectly expressed… Leaders should strive for authenticity over perfection. – **Sheryl Sandberg**

86. To have long term success as a coach or in any position of leadership, you have to be obsessed in some way. – **Pat Riley**

87. A man who wants to lead the orchestra must turn his back on the crowd. – **Max Lucado**

88. A person always doing his or her best becomes a natural leader, just by example. – **Joe DiMaggio**

89. In periods where there is no leadership, society stands still. Progress occurs when courageous, skillful leaders seize the opportunity to change things for the better. – **Harry Truman**

90. A genuine leader is not a searcher for consensus but a molder of consensus. – **Martin Luther King**

**Jr.**

91. All of the great leaders have had one characteristic in common: it was the willingness to confront unequivocally the major anxiety of their people in their time. This, and not much else, is the essence of leadership. – **John Kenneth Galbraith**

92. A leader is like a shepherd. He stays behind the flock, letting the most nimble go out ahead, whereupon the others follow, not realizing that all along they are being directed from behind. – **Nelson Mandela**

93. The art of leadership is saying no, not yes. It is very easy to say yes. – **Tony Blair**

94. Leadership consists of nothing but taking responsibility for everything that goes wrong and giving your subordinates credit for everything that goes well. – **Dwight D. Eisenhower**

95. If your actions inspire others to dream more, learn more, do more and become more, you are a leader. – **John Quincy Adams**

96. Leaders instill in their people a hope for success and a belief in themselves. Positive leaders empower people to accomplish their goals. – **Unknown**

97. The very essence of leadership is that you have to have vision. You can't blow an uncertain trumpet. – **Theodore M. Hesburgh**.

98. A good objective of leadership is to help those who are doing poorly to do well and to help those who are doing well to do even better. – **Jim Rohn**

99. The true mark of a leader is the willingness to stick with a bold course of action – an unconventional business strategy, a unique product– development roadmap, a controversial marketing campaign – even as the rest of the world wonders why you're not marching in step with the status quo. In other words, real leaders are happy to zig while others zag. They understand that in an era of hyper – competition and non– stop disruption, the only way to stand out from the crowd is to stand for something special. – **Bill Taylor**

100. Leaders think and talk about the solutions. Followers think and talk about the problems. – **Brian Tracy**

# POSITIVE QUOTES

1. All things are difficult before they are easy. – **Thomas Fuller**

2. A major factor in determining how our lives turn out is the way we choose to think. Everything that goes on inside the human mind in the form of thoughts, ideas, and information forms our personal philosophy. – **Jim Rohn**

3. It's only the person who's able to see beyond what things are at the moment to what things can be that truly deserves to be called a positive thinker. – **Don McArt**

4. Optimism is a happiness magnet. If you stay positive, good things and good people will be drawn to you. – **Mary Lou Retton**

5. Once you replace negative thoughts with positive ones, you'll start having positive results. – **Willie Nelson**

6. Start each day with a positive thought and a grateful

heart. – **Roy T. Bennett**

7. You are the only one who can control the way you think. Make sure you nourish the positive thoughts, and weed out the negative ones! – **Catherine Pulsifer**

8. Yesterday is not ours to recover, but tomorrow is ours to win or lose. – **Lyndon B. Johnson**

9. Work hard for what you want because it won't come to you without a fight. You have to be strong and courageous and know that you can do anything you put your mind to. If somebody puts you down or criticizes you, just keep on believing in yourself and turn it into something positive. – **Leah LaBelle**

10. The past has no power over the present moment. – **Eckhart Tolle**

11. One of the most efficient ways you can improve your life is by simply thinking in a more positive way. – **Robert Norman**

12. Love yourself. It is important to stay positive because beauty comes from the inside out. – **Jenn Proske**

13. The more positive thoughts you have, the better you feel, which causes you to have more positive thoughts, then you feel even better. – **James Borg,**

14. I think that life is difficult. People have challenges. Family members get sick, people get older, you don't always get the job or the promotion that you want. You have conflicts in your life. And really, life is about your resilience and your ability to go through your life and all of the ups and downs with a positive attitude. – **Jennifer Hyman**

15. Much of our pain or misery in life stems from our own outlook towards the situation. A paralyzed person can also be happy, so can be a financially poor family. – **Amit Ahlawat**

16. Either you run the day or the day runs you. – **Jim Rohn**

17. In order to carry a positive action we must develop here a positive vision. – **Dalai Lama**

18. I've always believed that you can think positive just as well as you can think negative. – **James A. Baldwin**

19. A positive attitude causes a chain reaction of positive thoughts, events and outcomes. It is a catalyst and it sparks extraordinary results. – **Wade Boggs**

20. You cannot have a positive life and a negative mind. – **Joyce Meyer**

21. I always like to look on the optimistic side of life, but I am realistic enough to know that life is a complex matter. – **Walt Disney**

22. Your hardest times often lead to the greatest moments of your life. Keep going. Tough situations build strong people in the end. – **Roy T. Bennett**

23. Don't forget to tell yourself positive things daily! You must love yourself internally to glow externally. – **Hannah Bronfman**

24. If opportunity doesn't knock, build a door. – **Milton Berle**

25. Positive thinking will let you do everything better than negative thinking will. – **Zig Ziglar**

26. We are all here for some special reason. Stop being a prisoner of your past. Become the architect of your future. – **Robin S. Sharma**

27. Pessimism leads to weakness, optimism to power. – **William James**

28. Always turn a negative situation into a positive situation. – **Michael Jordan**

29. You can't make positive choices for the rest of your life without an environment that makes those

choices easy, natural, and enjoyable. – **Deepak Chopra**

30. Today's a great day to change a life. Starting with yours. – **Robin Sharma**

31. The best revenge is massive success. – **Frank Sinatra**

32. The thing that lies at the foundation of positive change, the way I see it, is service to a fellow human being. – **Lee Iacocca**

33. Successful people maintain a positive focus in life no matter what is going on around them. They stay focused on their past successes rather than their past failures, and on the next action steps they need to take to get them closer to the fulfillment of their goals rather than all the other distractions that life presents to them. – **Jack Canfield**

34. If we're growing, we're always going to be out of our comfort zone. – **John C. Maxwell**

35. I am happy every day, because life is moving in a very positive way. – **Lil Yachty**

36. Positive thinking is more than just a tagline. It changes the way we behave. And I firmly believe that when I am positive, it not only makes me better, but it also makes those around me better. –

**Harvey Mackay**

37. There are always flowers for those who want to see them. – **Henri Matisse**

38. In every day, there are 1,440 minutes. That means we have 1,440 daily opportunities to make a positive impact. – **Les Brown**

39. I truly believe that everything that we do and everyone that we meet is put in our path for a purpose. There are no accidents; we're all teachers – if we're willing to pay attention to the lessons we learn, trust our positive instincts and not be afraid to take risks or wait for some miracle to come knocking at our door. – **Marla Gibbs**

40. The difference between a successful person and others is not a lack of strength, not a lack of knowledge, but rather a lack in will. – **Vince Lombardi**

41. I realized that if my thoughts immediately affect my body, I should be careful about what I think. Now if I get angry, I ask myself why I feel that way. If I can find the source of my anger, I can turn that negative energy into something positive. – **Yoko Ono**

42. I'm a very positive thinker, and I think that is what helps me the most in difficult moments. – **Roger**

**Federer**

43. If you realized how powerful your thoughts are, you would never think a negative thought. – **Peace Pilgrim**

44. Perpetual optimism is a force multiplier. – **Colin Powell**

45. Hope is a waking dream. – **Aristotle**

46. Focus on your strengths, not your weaknesses. Focus on your character, not your reputation. Focus on your blessings, not your misfortunes. – **Roy T. Bennett**

47. In times of great stress or adversity, it's always best to keep busy, to plow your anger and your energy into something positive. – **Lee Iacocca**

48. Attitude is a little thing that makes a big difference. – **Winston Churchill**

49. Positivity always wins…Always. – **Gary Vaynerchuk**

50. Choosing to be positive and having a grateful attitude is going to determine how you're going to live your life. – **Joel Osteen**

51. Few things in the world are more powerful than a

positive push. A smile. A world of optimism and hope. A 'you can do it' when things are tough. – **Richard M. DeVos**

52. You just keep a positive attitude no matter what comes in your way – challenges, roadblocks – don't let it faze you, and you can overcome anything. – **Rose Namajunas**

53. Change may not always bring growth, but there is no growth without change. – **Roy T. Bennett**

54. Nurture your mind with great thoughts, for you will never go any higher than you think. – **Benjamin Disraeli**

55. I am the greatest, I said that even before I knew I was. – **Muhammad Ali**

56. Stay positive and happy. Work hard and don't give up hope. Be open to criticism and keep learning. Surround yourself with happy, warm and genuine people. – **Tena Desae**

57. Stay positive in every situation and everything you do, never stop trying, have faith don't stop due to failure. – **Anurag Prakash Ray**

58. The only way of finding the limits of the possible is by going beyond them into the impossible. – **Arthur C. Clarke**

59. Be thankful for everything that happens in your life; it's all an experience. – **Roy T. Bennett**

60. A strong positive mental attitude will create more miracles than any wonder drug. – **Patricia Neal**

61. At the end of the day, the most overwhelming key to a child's success is the positive involvement of parents. – **Jane D. Hull**

62. All I can control is myself and just keep having a positive attitude. – **Rose Namajunas**

63. It is said that the darkest hour of the night comes just before the dawn. – **Thomas Fuller**

64. What you feel inside reflects on your face. So be happy and positive all the time. – **Sridevi**

65. If you absolutely can't stay positive, don't go negative, just cruise neutral for a while until you can get back up. – **Terri Guillemets**

66. Virtually nothing is impossible in this world if you just put your mind to it and maintain a positive attitude. – **Lou Holtz**

67. Positive thinking is like fuel to the car. It will keep you energized throughout your work.– **Abder–Rahman Ali**

68. If you have a positive attitude and constantly strive to give your best effort, eventually you will overcome your immediate problems and find you are ready for greater challenges. **– Pat Riley**

69. Live life to the fullest, and focus on the positive. – **Matt Cameron**

70. Wherever you go, no matter what the weather, always bring your own sunshine. – **Anthony J. D'Angelo**

71. Be the reason someone smiles. Be the reason someone feels loved and believes in the goodness in people. – **Roy T. Bennett**

72. Be positive with every idea surrounding your dreams. Think about the possibility of what you plan to do and approach it with an optimistic action. Stay positively. – **Israelmore Ayivor**

73. If you have a positive attitude and constantly strive to give your best effort, eventually you will overcome your immediate problems and find you are ready for greater challenges. – **Pat Riley**

74. No matter what you're going through, there's a light at the end of the tunnel and it may seem hard to get to it but you can do it and just keep working towards it and you'll find the positive side of things.

**– Demi Lovato**

75. Positive thinking is one of the most important aspects of success. If you want to be successful, you have to start with positive thinking, developing self–confidence, and, above all, self– responsibility. **– Bill McDowell**

76. Whether you believe or not, negative and positive thinking is infectious, as it tends to influence not only situations but also people around. **– Lindsay J. Hallie**

77. Say and do something positive that will help the situation; it doesn't take any brains to complain. **– Robert A. Cook**

78. Being in a positive state of mind is more important than you might think as the mind cannot be creative in a negative state. New ideas, thoughts and inspiration will only take place when the mind is positive. **– Joe Hinchliffe**

79. Once you replace negative thoughts with positive ones, you'll start having positive results. **– Willie Nelson**

80. There is a basic law that like attracts like. Negative thinking definitely attracts negative results. Conversely, if a person habitually thinks optimistically and hopefully, his positive thinking

sets in motion creative forces, and success instead of eluding him flows toward him. – **Norman Vincent Peale**

81. Research shows there is a strong correlation between positive feelings toward your job, and job performance and productivity. – **Reen Rose**

82. Train your mind to think positively. Try to have an optimistic outlook in the midst of a negative situation. – **Jonathan Brown**

83. That is what positive thinking is all about. It's about responding to life's obstacles with a positive, never – back– down attitude. – **Darrin Donnelly**

84. I personally believe that positive thinking creates a positive view toward life that can bring success and help lead a good, rich, healthy and happy life. – **Bill Mcdowell**

85. It's hard, but it's not as hard as you think if you think positive. – **Shirlene Cooper**

86. Affirmations are our mental vitamins, providing the supplementary positive thoughts we need to balance the barrage of negative events and thoughts we experience daily. – **Tia Walker**

87. When you consistently maintain a positive frame of mind, you'll become known as a problem– solver

rather than a complainer. People avoid complainers. They seek out problem– solvers. – **Joseph Sommerville**

88. The most important things in life are your friends, family, health, good humor and a positive attitude towards life. If you have these then you have everything! – **Catherine Pulsifer**

89. You will hear people talk about their problems so much at times but this is the wrong thing to do. You have to concentrate on the positives. Place your attention on the good things that happened throughout the day. – **Tristan Jan Tizon**

90. Your circumstances may be uncongenial, but they shall not remain so if you only perceive an ideal and strive to reach it. You cannot travel within and stand still without. – **James Allen**

91. Now it stands to reason that a person who is thinking about a concrete and worthwhile goal is going to reach it, because that's what he's thinking about – and we become what we think about. Conversely, the person who has no goal, who doesn't know where he's going, and whose thoughts must therefore be thoughts of confusion, anxiety, fear, and worry will become what he thinks about. – **Earl Nightingale**

92. It takes but one positive thought when given a

chance to survive and thrive to overpower an entire army of negative thoughts. – **Robert H. Schuller**

93. The truly successful person who attracts blessings into his or her life thinks and acts positively. – **Paul and Tracey McManus**

94. Some people have a positive attitude towards life only when all is well. However, when the going gets tough, their attitude changes instantly, and they become very negative or are consumed with self pity. – **Catherine Pulsifer**

95. If you visualize the things you don't want, that's what you will anchor in your brain. So think positive to anchor the positive. If you imagine confidence and good relations they will come. – **David Valois**

96. We think positive thoughts and we become a positive person. – **Andrew Evans**

97. Positive thinking helps you stand back up again when you are knocked down by bad luck or negativity. – **Tom Laurie**

98. The more you are positive and say, 'I want to have a good life,' the more you build that reality for yourself by creating the life that you want. – **Chris Pine**

99. I'm taking all the negatives in my life, and turning them into a positive. – **Pitbull**

100. I have never, ever focused on the negative of things. I always look at the positive. – **Sonia Sotomayor**

# SELF–DISCIPLINE QUOTES

1. Discipline is the bridge between goals and accomplishment. – **Jim Rohn**

2. Respect your efforts, respect yourself. Self–respect leads to self–discipline. When you have both firmly under your belt, that's real power. – **Clint Eastwood**

3. We do today what they won't, so tomorrow we can accomplish what they can't. – **Dwayne 'The Rock' Johnson**

4. Self–discipline is an act of cultivation. It requires you to connect today's actions to tomorrow's results. There's a season for sowing a season for reaping. Self–discipline helps you know which is which. – **Gary Ryan Blair**

5. Winners embrace hard work. They love the discipline of it, the trade–off they're making to win. Losers, on the other hand, see it as a punishment. And that's the difference. – **Lou Holtz**

6. In reading the lives of great men, I found that the

first victory they won was over themselves... self – discipline with all of them came first. – **Harry S Truman**

7. Discipline is the soul of an army. It makes small numbers formidable; procures success to the weak, and esteem to all. – **George Washington**

8. By constant self–discipline and self–control you can develop greatness of character. – **Grenville Kleiser**

9. A disciplined mind leads to happiness, and an undisciplined mind leads to suffering. – **Dalai Lama**

10. I think self–discipline is something, it's like a muscle. The more you exercise it, the stronger it gets. – **Daniel Goldstein**

11. Discipline is the refining fire by which talent becomes ability. – **Roy L. Smith**

12. Self–government won't work without self–discipline. – **Paul Harvey**

13. With self–discipline, most anything is possible. – **Theodore Roosevelt**

14. Self–discipline is what separates the winners and the losers. – **Thomas Peterffy**

15. If I want to be great I have to win the victory over myself…self–discipline. – **Harry S. Truman**

16. Self–denial and self–discipline, however, will be recognized as the outstanding qualities of a good soldier. – **William Lyon Mackenzie King**

17. We must all suffer one of two things: the pain of discipline or the pain of regret and disappointment. – **Jim Rohn**

18. Self–discipline is doing what needs to be done when it needs to be done even when you don't feel like doing it. – **Anonymous**

19. By constant self–discipline and self–control you can develop greatness of character. – **Grenville Kleiser**

20. Self–command is the main discipline. – **Ralph Waldo Emerson**

21. Discipline is the bridge between goals and accomplishments. – **Jim Rohn**

22. Without self–discipline, success is impossible, period. – **Lou Holtz**

23. He who lives without discipline dies without honor. – **Icelandic Proverb**

24. The ability to discipline yourself to delay

gratification in the short term in order to enjoy greater rewards in the long term is the indispensable prerequisite for success. – **Maxwell Maltz**

25. The price of excellence is discipline. The cost of mediocrity is disappointment. – **William Arthur Ward**

26. One discipline always leads to another discipline. – **Jim Rohn**

27. You have power over your mind, not outside events. Realize this, and you will find strength. – **Marcus Aurelius**

28. Self–discipline is the No.1 delineating factor between the rich, the middle class, and the poor. – **Robert Kiyosaki**

29. The pain of self–discipline will never be as great as the pain of regret. – **Anonymous**

30. A great way to develop self–discipline is to make it a habit to do the things you should be doing when you feel the laziest. Every time you feel really lazy, do the opposite of what you feel like doing. – **Anonymous**

31. Success is a matter of understanding and religiously practicing specific simple habits that always lead to success. – **Robjert J. Ringer**

32. Discipline not desire determines your destiny. – **Anonymous**

33. Confidence comes from discipline and training. – **Robert Kiyosaki**

34. Success doesn't just happen. You have to be intentional about it, and that takes discipline. – **John C. Maxwell**

35. Self–discipline is that which, next to virtue, truly and essentially raises one man above another. – **Joseph Addison**

36. No man is fit to command another that cannot command himself. – **William Penn**

37. Most talk about 'super– geniuses' is nonsense. I have found that when 'stars' drop out, successors are usually at hand to fill their places, and the successors are merely men who have learned by application and self–discipline to get full production from an average, normal brain. – **Charles M. Schwab**

38. Self–discipline is a form of freedom. Freedom from laziness and lethargy, freedom from the expectations and demands of others, freedom from weakness and fear – and doubt. Self–discipline allows a person to feel his individuality, his inner

strength, his talent. He is the master of, rather than a slave to, his thoughts and emotions. – **H. A. Dorfman**

39. Discipline is the foundation of a successful and happy life. – **Anonymous**

40. Self–discipline is the only power which can keep you energized even in the toughest of the circumstances. – **Sukant Ratnakar**

41. True freedom is impossible without a mind made free by discipline. – **Mortimer J. Adler**

42. Self–control is the chief element in self–respect, and self–respect is the chief element in courage. – **Thucydides**

43. We all have dreams. But in order to make dreams come into reality, it takes an awful lot of determination, dedication, self–discipline, and effort. – **Jesse Owens**

44. Self–discipline begins with the mastery of your thoughts. If you don't control what you think, you can't control what you do. Simply, self–discipline enables you to think first and act afterward. **Napoleon Hill**

45. Great leaders always have self–discipline – without exception. – **John C. Maxwell**

46. I could only achieve success in my life through self–discipline, and I applied it until my wish and my will became one. – **Nikola Tesla**

47. Self–discipline is a key to many doors. Not least of which is one that leads to a better, stronger, and healthier version of yourself. – **Zero Dean**

48. Self– respect is the fruit of discipline; the sense of dignity grows with the ability to say no to oneself. – **Abraham J. Heschel**

49. With this magic ingredient, you can accomplish anything and everything you want to, and it is called self–discipline. – **Brian Tracy**

50. Happiness is dependent on self–discipline. We are the biggest obstacles to our own happiness. It is much easier to do battle with society and with others than to fight our own nature. – **Dennis Prager**

51. Self–discipline equates to self–control. Your ability to control yourself and your actions, control what you say and do, and ensure that your behaviors are consistent with long– term goals and objectives is the mark of a superior person. – **Brian Tracy**

52. Do not bite at the bait of pleasure till you know there is no hook beneath it. – **Thomas Jefferson**

53. Mental toughness is many things and rather difficult to explain. Its qualities are sacrifice and self–denial. Also, most importantly, it is combined with a perfectly disciplined will that refuses to give in. It's a state of mind– you could call it character in action. – **Vince Lombardi**

54. All successes begin with self–discipline. It starts with you. – **Dwayne Johnson**

55. The future depends on what we do in the present. – **Mahatma Ghandi**

56. Success is actually a short race – a sprint fueled by discipline just long enough for habit to kick in and take over. – **Gary Keller**

57. With self–discipline most anything is possible. – **Theodore Roosevelt**

58. . By constant self–discipline and self–control you can develop greatness of character. – **Grenville Kleiser**

59. Willpower is what separates us from the animals. It's the capacity to restrain our impulses, resist temptation – do what's right and good for us in the long run, not what we want to do right now. It's central, in fact, to civilization. – **Dr. Roy Baumeister, Ph.D.**

60. He who cannot obey himself will be commanded. That is the nature of living creatures. – **Friedrich Nietzsche**

61. It doesn't matter whether you are pursuing success in business, sports, the arts, or life in general: The bridge between wishing and accomplishing is discipline.– **Harvey Mackay**

62. It is not enough to have great qualities; We should also have the management of them. – **La Rochefoucauld**

63. In essence, if we want to direct our lives, we must take control of our consistent actions. It's not what we do once in a while that shapes our lives, but what we do consistently. – **Tony Robbins**

64. Discipline really means our ability to get ourselves to do things when we don't want to. – **Arden Mahlberg**

65. Your ability to discipline yourself to set clear goals, and then to work toward them every day, will do more to guarantee your success than any other single factor. – **Brian Tracy**

66. He who is living without discipline is exposed to grievous ruin ... Who hath a harder battle to fight than he who striveth for self–mastery? And should

be our endeavor, even to master self, and thus daily to grow stronger than self and go on unto perfections. **– Thomas à Kempis**

67. Self–discipline is about controlling your desires and impulses while staying focused on what needs to get done to achieve your goal. **– Adam Sicinski**

68. You will never have a greater or lesser dominion than that over yourself ... the height of a man's success is gauged by his self–mastery; the depth of his failure by his self– abandonment ... And this law is the expression of eternal justice. He who cannot establish dominion over himself will have no dominion over others. **– Leonardo da Vinci**

69. Discipline yourself to do the things you need to do when you need to do them, and the day will come when you will be able to do the things you want to do when you want to do them. **– Zig Ziglar**

70. The difference between great people and everyone else is that great people create their lives actively, while everyone else is created by their lives, passively waiting to see where life takes them next. The difference between the two is the difference between living fully and just existing. **– Michael E. Gerberon**

71. Self– discipline is that which, next to virtue, truly and essentially raises one man above another. –

**Joseph Addison**

72. You can never conquer the mountain. You can only conquer yourself. – **Jim Whittaker**

73. I count him braver who overcomes his desires than him who conquers his enemies; for the hardest victory is over self. – **Aristotle**

74. Talent without discipline is like an octopus on roller skates. There's plenty of movement, but you never know if it's going to be forward, backwards, or sideways. – **H. Jackson Brown, Jr.**

75. The more disciplined you become, the easier life gets. – **Steve Pavlina**

76. Discipline without freedom is tyranny. Freedom without discipline is chaos. – **Cullen Hightower**

77. Self–respect is the fruit of discipline; the sense of dignity grows with the ability to say no to oneself. – **Abraham J. Heschel**

78. Self–discipline is the ability to make yourself do what you should do, when you should do it, whether you feel like it or not. – **Elbert Hubbard**

79. The individual who wants to reach the top in business must appreciate the might and force of habit. He must be quick to break those habits that

can break him– and hasten to adopt those practices that will become the habits that help him achieve the success he desires. – **J. Paul Getty**

80. In reading the lives of great men, I found that the first victory they won was over themselves…self – discipline with all of them came first. – **Harry S. Truman**

81. If it were easy to walk the path of self– discipline, we wouldn't gain much from it. – **Glenn C. Stewart**

82. A man without decision of character can never be said to belong to himself… He belongs to whatever can make captive of him. – **John Foster**

83. Discipline is built by consistently performing small acts of courage. – **Robin Sharma**

84. We are what we repeatedly do, excellence then is not an act, but a habit. – **Aristotle**

85. Discipline is the ability to control our conduct by principle rather than by social pressure. – **Glenn C. Stewart**

86. If we don't discipline ourselves, the world will do it for us. – **William Feather**

87. . Self–discipline is a self–enlarging process. – **M.**

**Scott Peck**

88. Self–respect is the fruit of discipline; the sense of dignity grows with the ability to say no to oneself. – **Abraham J. Heschel**

89. We don't have to be smarter than the rest; we have to be more disciplined than the rest. – **Warren Buffett**

90. Self– discipline is about controlling your desires and impulses while staying focused on what needs to get done to achieve your goal. – **Adam Sicinski**

91. Willpower and self–discipline are more effective than intellect and talent.– **Akiroq Brost**

92. Discipline is the silent force at work that breeds success. It requires only one thing; that you sacrifice time in things you enjoy. – **Anonymous**

93. If the self–discipline of the free cannot match the iron discipline of the mailed fist– in economic, political, scientific and all other kinds of struggles as well as the military – then the peril to freedom will continue to rise. – **John F. Kennedy**

94. It is often the simple daily practices that influence our lives in dramatic ways. – **Alaric Hutchinson**

95. Discipline really means our ability to get ourselves

to do things when we don't want to. – **Arden Mahlberg**

96. Discipline is choosing between what you want now and what you want most. – **Abrahm Lincoln**

97. Small disciplines repeated with consistency every day lead to great achievements gained slowly over time. – **John C. Maxwell**

98. The great master key to riches is nothing more or less than the self–discipline necessary to help you take full and complete possession of your own mind. – **Napoleon Hill**

99. Success is created through the performance of a few small daily disciplines that stack up over time to produce achievements far beyond anything you could of ever planned for. Failure, on the other hand, is just as easy to slip into. Failure's is nothing more than the inevitable outcome of a few small acts of daily neglect performed consistently over time so that they take you past the point of no return. – **Robin Sharma**

100. Find what you love to do, and go do it. You will never be successful until you have a plan, and the discipline and determination to go through with that plan. – **Julius Williams**

# FUNNY QUOTES

1.  My doctor gave me six months to live, but when I couldn't pay the bill he gave me six months more. – **Walter Matthau**

2.  If you think nobody cares if you're alive, try missing a couple of car payments. – **Earl Wilson**

3.  Why do they call it "rush hour" when nothing moves? – **Robin Williams**

4.  I changed all my passwords to 'Incorrect.' So whenever I forget, it will tell me 'Your password is incorrect. – **Michael Scott**

5.  Put your hand on a hot stove for a minute, and it seems like an hour. Sit with a pretty girl for an hour, and it seems like a minute. That's relativity. – **Albert Einstein**

6.  No man has a good enough memory to be a successful liar. – **Abraham Lincoln**

7.  Cleaning up with children around is like shoveling during a blizzard. – **Margaret Culkin Banning**

8.  A bank is a place that will lend you money if you can prove that you don't need it. **– Bob Hope**

9.  The real trouble with reality is that there is no background music. – **Anonymous**

10. My therapist told me the way to achieve true inner peace is to finish what I start. So far I've finished two bags of M&Ms and a chocolate cake. I feel better already. – **Dave Barry**

11. I intend to live forever. So far, so good. – **Steven Wright**

12. Expecting the world to treat you fairly because you are a good person is a little like expecting the bull not to attack you because you are a vegetarian. – **Dennis Wholey**

13. The reason so few people are successful is no one has yet found a way for someone to sit down and slide uphill. – **W. Clement Stone**

14. Tomorrow is often the busiest day of the week. – **Spanish proverb**

15. I need a six month vacation twice a year. – **Anonymous**

16. Always forgive your enemies; nothing annoys them so much. – **Oscar Wilde**

17. The best way to teach your kids about taxes is by eating 30 percent of their ice cream. – **Bill Murray**

18. The best way to appreciate your job is to imagine yourself without one. – **Oscar Wilde**

19. Never trust people who smile constantly. They're either selling something or not very bright. – **Laurell K. Hamilton**

20. If at first you don't succeed, destroy all evidence that you tried. – **Steven Wright**

21. The difference between stupidity and genius is that genius has its limits. – **Albert Einstein**

22. The trouble with being in the rat race is that even if you win, you're still a rat. – **Lily Tomlin**

23. The only way to keep your health is to eat what you don't want, drink what you don't like, and do what you'd rather not. – **Mark Twain**

24. Never try to teach a pig to sing; it wastes your time and it annoys the pig. **– Robert A. Heinlein**

25. For a politician to complain about the press is like a ship's captain complaining about the sea. **Enoch Powell**

26. The best things in life are free. The second best are very expensive. – **Coco Chanel**

27. Many people lose their tempers merely from seeing you keep yours. – **Frank Moore Colby**

28. I wish people who have trouble communicating would just shut up. – **Tom Lehrer**

29. The road to success is dotted with many tempting parking spaces. – **Will Rogers**

30. People often say that motivation doesn't last. Well, neither does bathing – that's why we recommend it daily. – **Zig Ziglar**

31. I believe in the discipline of silence, and could talk for hours about it. – **George Bernard Shaw**

32. What a kid I got, I told him about the birds and the bees and he told me about the butcher and my wife. – **Rodney Dangerfield**

33. Money can't buy you happiness but it does bring you a more pleasant form of misery. – **Spike Milligan**

34. You can't have everything. Where would you put it? – **Steven Wright**

35. Everybody talks about the weather, but nobody does

anything about it. – **Charles Dudley Warner**

36. If you think you are too small to make a difference, try sleeping with a mosquito**. – Dalai Lama**

37. Do not argue with an idiot. He will drag you down to his level and beat you with experience. – **Greg King**

38. A successful man is one who makes more money than his wife can spend. A successful woman is one who can find such a man. – **Lana Turner**

39. I used to think I was indecisive, but now I'm not so sure. – **Unknown**

40. It took me fifteen years to discover I had no talent for writing, but I couldn't give it up because by then I was too famous. – **Robert Benchley**

41. Don't worry about the world coming to an end today. It's already tomorrow in Australia." – **Charles Schulz**

42. Due to budget cuts the light at the end of the tunnel has been turned off. – **Aaron Paul**

43. If you let your head get too big, it'll break your neck. – **Elvis Presley**

44. Monday is an awful way to spend 1/7 of your life. –

– **Steven Wright**

45. One advantage of talking to yourself is that you know at least somebody's listening. – **Franklin P. Jones**

46. If you think your boss is stupid, remember: you wouldn't have a job if he was any smarter. – **John Gotti**

47. I'd kill for a Nobel Peace Prize. – **Steven Wright**

48. If I had asked people what they wanted, they would have said faster horses. – **Henry Ford**

49. Sell a man a fish, he eats for a day. Teach a man to fish, you ruin a wonderful business opportunity. – **Karl Marx**

50. I like work; it fascinates me. I can sit and look at it for hours. – **Jerome K. Jerome**

51. There are two kinds of people: those who do the work and those who take the credit. Try to be in the first group; there is less competition there. – **Indira Gandhi**

52. If hard work is the key to success, most people would rather pick the lock. – **Claude McDonald**

53. The closest to perfection a person ever comes is

when he fills out a job application form. – **Stanley J. Randall**

54. When you see a married couple walking down the street, the one that's a few steps ahead is the one that's mad. – **Helen Rowland**

55. Inside me there's a thin person struggling to get out, but I can usually sedate him with four or five cupcakes. – **Bob Thaves**

56. Light travels faster than sound. This is why some people appear bright until they speak. – **Steven Wright**

57. The most important four words for a successful marriage: 'I'll do the dishes.' – **Anonymous**

58. I always give 100% at Work: 10% Monday, 23% Tuesday, 40% Wednesday, 22% Thursday, and 5% Friday. – **Anonymous**

59. My psychiatrist told me I was crazy and I said I want a second opinion. He said okay, you're ugly too. – **Rodney Dangerfield**

60. Friendship is like peeing on yourself: everyone can see it, but only you get the warm feeling that it brings. – **Robert Bloch**

61. When I hear somebody sigh, "Life is hard", I am

always tempted to ask, "Compared to what?" – **Sydney Harris**

62. When I die, I want to go peacefully like my grandfather did–in his sleep. Not yelling and screaming like the passengers in his car. – **Bob Monkhouse**

63. The best way to get most husbands to do something is to suggest that perhaps they're too old to do it. – **Ann Bancroft**

64. My Favorite Machine At The Gym Is The Vending – **Machine. Caroline Rhea**

65. Why do people say "no offense" right before they're about to offend you? – **Anonymous**

66. I want my children to have all the things I couldn't afford. Then I want to move in with them. – **Phyllis Diller**

67. By all means, marry. If you get a good wife, you'll become happy; if you get a bad one, you'll become a philosopher. – **Socrates**

68. If you steal from one author, it's plagiarism; if you steal from many, it's research. – **Wilson Mizner**

69. According to most studies, people's number one fear is public speaking. Number two is death. Death

is number two! Does that sound right? That means to the average person, if you go to a funeral, you're better off in the casket than doing the eulogy. – **Jerry Seinfeld**

70. Life expectancy would grow by leaps and bounds if green vegetables smelled as good as bacon. – **Doug Larson**

71. "Consider the postage stamp: its usefulness consists in the ability to stick to one thing 'til it gets there. – **Josh Billings**

72. If you want your children to listen, try talking softly – to someone else. – **Ann Landers**

73. Money won't make you happy … but everybody wants to find out for themselves. – **Zig Ziglar**

74. Have you ever noticed that anybody driving slower than you is an idiot, and anyone going faster than you is a maniac? – **George Carlin**

75. When a man opens a car door for his wife, it's either a new car or a new wife. – **Prince Philip**

76. Life is hard; it's harder if you're stupid. – **John Wayne**

77. Laughing at our mistakes can lengthen our own life. Laughing at someone else's can shorten it. – **Cullen**

**Hightower**

78. If you could kick the person in the pants responsible for most of your trouble, you wouldn't sit for a month. – **Theodore Roosevelt**

79. Today I saw something through a store window that was truly stunning, beautiful and sexy. I wanted to get it for you, but then I realized it's my own reflection! – **Anonymous**

80. I don't want any yes– men around me. I want everybody to tell me the truth even if it costs them their job. – **Samuel Goldwyn**

81. A computer once beat me at chess, but it was no match for me at kickboxing. – **Emo Philips**

82. A lie gets halfway around the world before the truth has a chance to get its pants on. – **Winston Churchill**

83. My wife dresses to kill. She cooks the same way. – **Henny Youngman**

84. It does not matter whether you win or lose, what matters is whether I win or lose! – **Steven Weinberg**

85. I think I'm starting to have a problem with my vision, ever since I got married I haven't seen any

money through the entire house. – (**unknown**)

86. I don't know if my husband dreams in color, but he snores in Dolby. – **Melanie White**

87. I now pronounce you man and wife, you may now change your Facebook status. – **Anonymous**

88. The best way to remember your wife's birthday is to forget it once. – **Ogden Nash**

89. My doctor told me that jogging could add years to my life. I think he was right. I feel ten years older already. – **Milton Berle**

90. Only two things are infinite, the universe and human stupidity, and I'm not sure about the former. – **Albert Einstein**

91. It's only when you look at an ant through a magnifying glass on a sunny day that you realize how often they burst into flames. – **Harry Hill**

92. Most people work just hard enough not to get fired and get paid just enough money not to quit. – **George Carlin**

93. What the world needs is more geniuses with humility; there are so few of us left. – **Oscar Levant**

94. The two most common elements in the universe are hydrogen and stupidity. – **Harlan Ellison**

95. Before marriage, a man declares that he would lay down his life to serve you; after marriage, he won't even lay down his newspaper to talk to you. – **Helen Rowland**

96. It's amazing that the amount of news that happens in the world every day always just exactly fits the newspaper. – **Jerry Seinfeld**

97. I told my psychiatrist that everyone hates me. He said I was being ridiculous – everyone hasn't met me yet. – **Rodney Dangerfield**.

98. I am not a vegetarian because I love animals; I am a vegetarian because I hate plants. – **A. Whitney Brown**

99. Two golden rules to a Happy Marriage: 1– The wife is always right. 2– When you feel she is wrong slap yourself and Read rule number 1 again. –( **unknown)**

100. Marriage is a bond between a person who never remembers anniversaries and another who never forgets them. – **( anonymous)**

# FINANCE QUOTES

1.  Money is a great servant but a bad master.– **Francis Bacon**

2.  The only way you will ever permanently take control of your financial life is to dig deep and fix the root problem**. – Suze Orman**

3.  Your net worth to the world is usually determined by what remains after your bad habits are subtracted from your good ones. – **Benjamin Franklin**

4.  You don't want to have so much money going toward your mortgage every month that you can't enjoy life or take care of your other financial responsibilities. – **Dave Ramsey**

5.  Frugality includes all the other virtues. – **Cicero**

6.  Before you speak, listen. Before you write, think. Before you spend, earn. Before you invest, investigate. Before you criticize, wait. Before you pray, forgive. Before you quit, try. Before you retire, save. Before you die, give. – **William Arthur Ward**

7. Opportunity is missed by most people because it is dressed in overalls and looks like work. – **Thomas Edison**

8. Empty pockets never held anyone back. Only empty heads and empty hearts can do that. – **Norman Vincent Peale**

9. An investment in knowledge pays the best interest. – **Benjamin Franklin**

10. The rich invest their money and spend what is left; the poor spend their money and invest what is left. – **Jim Rohn**

11. How many millionaires do you know who have become wealthy by investing in savings accounts? I rest my case. – **Robert G. Allen**

12. I never attempt to make money on the stock market. I buy on the assumption that they could close the market the next day and not reopen it for ten years. – **Warren Buffett**

13. Money you won't need to use for at least seven years is money for investing. The goal here is to have your account grow over time to help you finance a distant goal, such as building a retirement fund. Since your goal is in the future, money for investing belongs in stocks. – **Suze Orman**

14. Never depend on single income. Make investment to create a second source. – **Warren Buffett**

15. Many people take no care of their money till they come nearly to the end of it, and others do just the same with their time. – **Johann Wolfgang von Goethe**

16. It's good to have money and the things that money can buy, but it's good, too, to check up once in a while and make sure that you haven't lost the things that money can't buy. – **George Lorimer**

17. You can only become truly accomplished at something you love. Don't make money your goal. Instead, pursue the things you love doing, and then do them so well that people can't take their eyes off you. – **Maya Angelou**

18. Money is only a tool. It will take you wherever you wish, but it will not replace you as the driver. – **Ayn Rand**

19. In the absence of the gold standard, there is no way to protect savings from confiscation through inflation. There is no safe store of value. – **Alan Greenspan**

20. Rule No. 1: Never lose money. Rule No. 2: Never forget Rule No. 1. – **Warren Buffett**

21. Financial peace isn't the acquisition of stuff. It's learning to live on less than you make, so you can give money back and have money to invest. You can't win until you do this. – **Dave Ramsey**

22. Don't gamble; take all your savings and buy some good stock and hold it till it goes up, then sell it. If it don't go up, don't buy it. – **Will Rogers**

23. Buy when everyone else is selling and hold until everyone else is buying. That's not just a catchy slogan. It's the very essence of successful investing. – **J. Paul Getty**

24. If you're good at something, never do it for free. – **Jonathan Nolan**

25. Being rich is a good thing. Not just in the obvious sense of benefitting you and your family, but in the broader sense. Profits are not a zero sum game. The more you make, the more of a financial impact you can have. – **Mark Cuban**

26. Invest in as much of yourself as you can, you are your own biggest asset by far. – **Warren Buffett**

27. Surplus wealth is a sacred trust which its possessor is bound to administer in his lifetime for the good of the community. – **Andrew Carnegie**

28. Money can't buy happiness, but it will certainly get

you a better class of memories. – **Ronald Reagan**

29. He who loses money, loses much; He who loses a friend, loses much more; He who loses faith, loses all. – **Eleanor Roosevelt**

30. The real measure of your wealth is how much you'd be worth if you lost all your money. – **Anonymous**

31. When you're building a company, you need to continually strengthen every component – finance, strategic partnerships, executive team, and relationships with every last constituency. – **Michael J. Saylor**

32. Formal education will make you a living. Self–education will make you a fortune. – **Jim Rohn**

33. Security depends not so much upon how much you have, as upon how much you can do without. – **Joseph Wood Krutch**

34. The people who know personal finance hide the money very carefully. – **James Altucher**

35. Never spend your money before you have earned it.– **Thomas Jefferson**

36. It is incumbent upon each of us to improve spending and savings practices to ensure our own individual financial security and preserve the

collective economic well– being of our great society. – **Ron Lewis**

37. Wealth after all is a relative thing since he that has little and wants less is richer than he that has much and wants more. – **Charles Caleb Colton**

38. The way to stop financial joyriding is to arrest the chauffeur, not the automobile. – **Woodrow Wilson**

39. If money is your hope for independence you will never have it. The only real security that a man will have in this world is a reserve of knowledge, experience, and ability. – **Henry Ford**

40. Happiness is not in the mere possession of money; it lies in the joy of achievement, in the thrill of creative effort. – **Franklin D. Roosevelt**

41. Too many people spend money they earned..to buy things they don't want..to impress people that they don't like. – **Will Rogers**

42. Every day is a bank account, and time is our currency. No one is rich, no one is poor, we've got 24 hours each. – **Christopher Rice**

43. It's not the employer who pays the wages. Employers only handle the money. It's the customer who pays the wages. – **Henry Ford**

44. Try to save something while your salary is small; it's impossible to save after you begin to earn more. **– Jack Benny**

45. Wealth consists not in having great possessions, but in having few wants**. – Epictetus**

46. Without continual growth and progress, such words as improvement, achievement, and success have no meaning**. – Benjamin Franklin**

47. It is time for us to stand and cheer for the doer, the achiever, the one who recognizes the challenge and does something about it. **– Vince Lombardi**

48. A wise person should have money in their head, but not in their heart. **– Jonathan Swift**

49. Wealth is the ability to fully experience life. **– Henry David Thoreau**

50. Money demands that you sell, not your weakness to men's stupidity, but your talent to their reason. **– Ayn Rand**

51. Don't tell me what you value, show me your budget, and I'll tell you what you value. **– Joe Biden**

52. We make a living by what we get, but we make a life by what we give. **– Winston Churchill**

53. Money can't buy you happiness but it does bring you a more pleasant form of misery. – **Spike Milligan**

54. It's not how much money you make, but how much money you keep, how hard it works for you, and how many generations you keep it for.– **Robert T. Kiyosaki**

55. I'm only rich because I know when I'm wrong…I basically have survived by recognizing my mistakes. – **George Soros**

56. The money you have gives you freedom; the money you pursue enslaves you. – **Jean Jacques Rousseau**

57. Wealth is like sea– water; the more we drink, the thirstier we become; and the same is true of fame. – – **Arthur Schopenhauer**

58. The individual investor should act consistently as an investor and not as a speculator. – **Ben Graham**

59. The stock market is filled with individuals who know the price of everything, but the value of nothing. – **Phillip Fisher**

60. I'm a great believer in luck, and I find the harder I work the more I have of it. – **Thomas Jefferson**

61. Wealth is not his that has it, but his that enjoys it. –

## Benjamin Franklin

62. Chase the vision, not the money. The money will end up following you. – **Tony Hsieh**

63. Early to bed and early to rise makes a man healthy, wealthy, and wise. – **Benjamin Franklin**

64. If we command our wealth, we shall be rich and free. If our wealth commands us, we are poor indeed. – **Edmund Burke**

65. It's simple arithmetic: Your income can grow only to the extent you do. – **T. Harv Eker**

66. You must gain control over your money or the lack of it will forever control you. – **Dave Ramsey**

67. Don't let the fear of losing be greater than the excitement of winning. – – **Robert Kiyosaki**

68. The Stock Market is designed to transfer money from the Active to the Patient. – **Warren Buffett**

69. Let him who would enjoy a good future waste none of his present. – **Roger Babson**

70. A real entrepreneur is somebody who has no safety net underneath them. – **Henry Kravis**

71. If you don't value your time, neither will others.

Stop giving away your time and talents. Value what you know & start charging for it. – **Kim Garst**

72. Where large sums of money are concerned, it is advisable to trust nobody. – **Agatha Christie**

73. Money and success don't change people; they merely amplify what is already there. – **Will Smith**

74. Time is more value than money. You can get more money, but you cannot get more time. – **Jim Rohn**

75. One of the funny things about the stock market is that every time one person buys, another sells, and both think they are astute. – **William Feather**

76. A successful man is one who can lay a firm foundation with the bricks others have thrown at him. – **David Brinkley**

77. I believe that through knowledge and discipline, financial peace is possible for all of us. –**Dave Ramsey**

78. The habit of saving is itself an education; it fosters every virtue, teaches self– denial, cultivates the sense of order, trains to forethought, and so broadens the mind. – **T.T. Munger**

79. A budget tells us what we can't afford, but it doesn't keep us from buying it. **William Feather**

80. My formula for success is rise early, work late and strike oil. – **JP Getty**

81. The thing I have discovered about working with personal finance is that the good news is that it is not rocket science. Personal finance is about 80 percent behavior. It is only about 20 percent head knowledge**. – Dave Ramsey**

82. It is not the man who has too little, but the man who craves more, that is poor. – **Seneca**

83. Never spend your money before you have it. – **Thomas Jefferson**

84. It's not the situation, but whether we react (negative) or respond (positive) to the situation that's important**. – Zig Ziglar**

85. Develop success from failures. Discouragement and failure are two of the surest stepping stones to success. – **Dale Carnegie**

86. If you're in the luckiest one per cent of humanity, you owe it to the rest of humanity to think about the other 99 per cent. – **Warren Buffett**

87. You don't have to be like most people around you, because most people never become truly rich and wealthy. – **Manoj Arora**

88. Invest in yourself. Your career is the engine of your wealth. **Paul Clitheroe**

89. An investment in knowledge pays the best interest. – **Benjamin Franklin**

90. What we really want to do is what we are really meant to do. When we do what we are meant to do, money comes to us, doors open for us, we feel useful, and the work we do feels like play to us. – **Julia Cameron**

91. It's good to have money and the things that money can buy, but it's good, too, to check up once in a while and make sure that you haven't lost the things that money can't buy. – **George Horace Lorimer**

92. Wealth consists not in having great possessions, but in having few wants. – **Epictetus**

93. A big part of financial freedom is having your heart and mind free from worry about the what– ifs of life. – **Suze Orman**

94. Finance is not merely about making money. It's about achieving our deep goals and protecting the fruits of our labor. It's about stewardship and, therefore, about achieving the good society. – **Robert J. Shiller**

95. Beware of little expenses; a small leak will sink a great ship. – **Benjamin Franklin**

96. Just because you can afford it doesn't mean you should buy it. – **Suze Orman**

97. It's not your salary that makes you rich, it's your spending habits. – **Charles Jaffe**

98. You attract poverty when you lack value for time – **Sunday Adelaja**

99. If you want your income to grow, you too must grow. –**Idowu Koyenikan**

100. You will either tell your money what to do, or the lack of it will always manage you. –**Dave Ramsey**

# LOVE QUOTES

1. The cure for all ills and wrongs, the cares, the sorrows and the crimes of humanity, all lie in the one word 'love.' It is the divine vitality that everywhere produces and restores life. – **Lydia Maria Child**

2. The greatest single cause of a poor self image is the absence of unconditional love. – **Zig Ziglar**

3. If you truly love your work, you'll do whatever it takes to master it. If you master it, you'll change the world. – **Maxime Lagacé**

4. I have decided to stick with love. Hate is too great a burden to bear. – **Martin Luther King, Jr.**

5. Love is the only sane and satisfactory answer to the problem of human existence. – **Erich Fromm**

6. The most important thing in life is to learn how to give out love, and to let it come in. – **Morrie Schwartz**

7. What a man thinks of himself, that it is which determines, or rather indicates his fate. – **Henry David Thoreau**

8. Love recognizes no barriers. It jumps hurdles, leaps fences, penetrates walls to arrive at its destination full of hope. – **Maya Angelou**

9. I believe that unarmed truth and unconditional love will have the final word in reality. This is why right, temporarily defeated, is stronger than evil triumphant. – **Martin Luther King Jr**

10. Patience is the mark of true love. If you truly love someone, you will be more patient with that person. – **Thich Nhat Hanh**

11. Love is of all passions the strongest, for it attacks simultaneously the head, the heart, and the senses. – **Lao Tzu**

12. I think what motivates people is not great hate, but great love for other people. – **Huey Newton**

13. You never lose by loving. You always lose by holding back. – **Barbara De Angelis**

14. Lots of people want to ride with you in the limo, but what you want is someone who will take the bus with you when the limo breaks down. – **Oprah Winfrey**

15. Love life and life will love you back. Love people and they will love you back. – **Arthur Rubinstein**

16. Darkness cannot drive out darkness; only light can do that. Hate cannot drive out hate, only love can do that. – **Martin Luther King Jr.**

17. Love cures people – both the ones who give it and the ones who receive it. **Karl Menninger**

18. You don't love someone because they're perfect, you love them in spite of the fact that they're not. – **Jodi Picoult**

19. One is loved because one is loved. No reason is needed for loving**. – Paulo Coelho**

20. There is only one happiness in life, to love and be loved. – **George Sand**

21. Love is a choice you make from moment to moment. **Barbara De Angelis**

22. When you arise in the morning, think of what a precious privilege it is to be alive – to breathe, to think, to enjoy, to love. – **Marcus Aurelius**

23. You must love in such a way that the person you love feels free. – **Thich Nhat Hanh**

24. Life is meaningless only if we allow it to be. Each of us has the power to give life meaning, to make our time and our bodies and our words into instruments of love and hope. – **Tom Head**

25. You have found true love when you realize that you want to wake up beside your love every morning even when you have your differences. – **Unknown**

26. Love is that condition in which the happiness of another person is essential to your own. – **Robert A. Heinlein**

27. Being deeply loved by someone gives you strength, while loving someone deeply gives you courage. – **Lao Tzu**

28. If you aren't good at loving yourself, you will have a difficult time loving anyone, since you'll resent the time and energy you give another person that you aren't even giving to yourself. – **Barbara De Angelis**

29. Love yourself first and everything else falls into line. You really have to love yourself to get anything done in this world. – **Lucille Ball**

30. Gravitation is not responsible for people falling in love. – **Albert Einstein**

31. "One word frees us of all the weight and pain in

life. That word is love!" –**Sophocles**

32. The good life is inspired by love and guided by knowledge. **Bertrand Russell**

33. I love you and that's the beginning and end of everything. – **F. Scott Fitzgerald**

34. We accept the love we think we deserve. – **Stephen Chbosky**

35. Love is never lost. If not reciprocated, it will flow back and soften and purify the heart. – **Washington Irving**

36. Keep love in your heart. A life without it is like a sunless garden when the flowers are dead**. – Oscar Wilde**

37. You know you're in love when you can't fall asleep because reality is finally better than your dreams. – **Dr. Seuss**

38. **We can** only learn to love by loving. – **Iris Murdoch**

39. Love the life you live. Live the life you love. – **Bob Marley**

40. Attention is the rarest and purest form of generosity. **Simone Weil**

41. Love is like the wind, you can't see it but you can feel it. – **Nicholas Sparks**

42. Kindness in words creates confidence. Kindness in thinking creates profundity. Kindness in giving creates love. **Lao Tzu**

43. There is never a time or place for true love. It happens accidentally, in a heartbeat, in a single flashing, throbbing moment. – **Sarah Dessen**

44. To love is, first of all, to accept ourselves as we actually are. **Thich Nhat Hanh**

45. The beautiful thing about love is that you just need to plant it once and nurture it and it shall bloom into blossoms that would cover the valleys." – **Hermann J. Steinherr**

46. Love is the absence of judgment. – **Dalai Lama XIV**

47. Unless you love someone, nothing else makes sense. **E.E. Cummings**

48. There can be no deep disappointment where there is not deep love. – **Martin Luther King, Jr**.

49. The world is too dangerous for anything but truth and too small for anything but love. – **William**

**Sloane Coffin**

50. It's better to have loved and lost than never to have loved at all. – **Alfred Tennyson**

51. Love must be as much a light as it is a flame. Henry **David Thoreau**

52. What can you do to promote world peace? Go home and love your family. – **Mother Teresa**

53. Where there is love there is life. – **Mahatma Gandhi**

54. Love yourself. Then forget it. Then, love the world. **Mary Oliver**

55. Love is not about how many days, weeks or months you've been together, it's all about how much you love each other every day. – **Unknown**

56. To the world you may be one person, but to one person you are the world. – **Bill Wilson**

57. A life lived in love will never be dull. Leo Buscaglia

58. Life without love is like a tree without blossoms or fruit. – **Khalil Gibran**

59. You call it madness, but I call it love. – **Don Byas**

60. The only thing we never get enough of is love; and the only thing we never give enough of is love.– **Henry Miller**

61. A flower cannot blossom without sunshine, and man cannot live without love." – **Max Muller**

62. Love is supposed to be based on trust, and trust on love, it's something rare and beautiful when people can confide in each other without fearing what the other person will think. — **E.A. Bucchianeri**

63. In the end we discover that to love and let go can be the same thing. – **Jack Kornfield**

64. Love grows by giving. The love we give away is the only love we keep. The only way to retain love is to give it away. – **Elbert Hubbard**

65. When the power of love overcomes the love of power the world will know peace. – **Jimi Hendrix**

66. Love is a great master. It teaches us to be what we never were. – **Moliere**

67. Givers need to set limits because takers rarely do. – **Rachel Wolchin**

68. Where there is great love, there are always miracles. – **Willa Cather**

69. Those who love deeply never grow old; they may die of old age, but they die young. **Sir Arthur Pinero**

70. A friend is someone who knows all about you and still loves you. **Elbert Hubbard**

71. The ultimate lesson all of us have to learn is unconditional love, which includes not only others but ourselves as well. **Elizabeth Kubler– Ross**

72. Self– care is never a selfish act – it is simply good stewardship of the only gift I have, the gift I was put on earth to offer to others**. Parker Palmer**

73. "It takes courage to love, but pain through love is the purifying fire which those who love generously know. We all know people who are so much afraid of pain that they shut themselves up like clams in a shell and, giving out nothing, receive nothing and therefore shrink until life is a mere living death." – **Eleanor Roosevelt**

74. Love many things, for therein lies the true strength, and whosoever loves much performs much, and can accomplish much, and what is done in love is done well. **Vincent van Gogh**

75. Just don't give up trying to do what you really want to do. Where there's love and inspiration, I don't

think you can go wrong. **Ella Fitzgerald**

76. Work without love is slavery. **Mother Teresa**

77. Love will find a way through paths where wolves fear to prey. – **Lord Byron**

78. I have found the paradox, that if you love until it hurts, there can be no more hurt, only more love. **Mother Teresa**

79. Love takes off masks that we fear we cannot live without and know we cannot live within.– **James Baldwin**

80. We are shaped and fashioned by what we love. – **Johann Wolfgang von Goethe**

81. One word frees us of all the weight and pain of life: That word is love. – **Sophocles**

82. It is better to have loved and lost than never to have loved at all.– **Samuel Butler**

83. There are two basic motivating forces: fear and love. When we are afraid, we pull back from life. When we are in love, we open to all that life has to offer with passion, excitement, and acceptance. – **John Lennon**

84. Love is a force more formidable than any other. It is

invisible – it cannot be seen or measured, yet it is powerful enough to transform you in a moment, and offer you more joy than any material possession could. – **Barbara De Angelis**

85. Love is a fabric which never fades, no matter how often it is washed in the water of adversity and grief**. – Robert Fulghum**

86. Everything is clearer when you're in love. – **John Lennon**

87. Let's practice motivation and love, not discrimination and hate**. Zendaya**

88. Love is like a beautiful flower which I may not touch, but whose fragrance makes the garden a place of delight just the same. – **Helen Keller**

89. Do what you love, and you will find the way to get it out to the world." – **Judy Collins**

90. Love is shown more in deeds than in words. – **Saint Ignatius**

91. Life is the first gift, love is the second, and understanding the third. – **Marge Piercy**

92. Love is more than a noun – it is a verb; it is more than a feeling – it is caring, sharing, helping, sacrificing. – **William Arthur Ward**

93. Let us always meet each other with smile, for the smile is the beginning of love. – **Mother Teresa**

94. Love is friendship that has caught fire. It is a quiet understanding, mutual confidence, sharing and forgiving. It is loyalty through good and bad times. It settles for less than perfection and makes allowances for human weaknesses. – **Ann Landers**

95. Love is the only force capable of transforming an enemy into friend. – **Martin Luther King, Jr.**

96. You will find as you look back upon your life that the moments when you have truly lived are the moments when you have done things in the spirit of love.– **Henry Drummond**

97. Love and compassion are necessities, not luxuries. Without them humanity cannot survive.– **Dalai Lama**

98. The more one judges, the less one loves.– **Honoré de Balzac**

99. The first duty of love is to listen. – **Paul Tillich**

100. Love cures people– both the ones who give it and the ones who receive it. – **Karl A. Menninger**

# CONFIDENCE QUOTES

1. Our deepest fear is not that we are inadequate. Our deepest fear is that we are powerful beyond measure. It is our light, not our darkness that most frightens us. We ask ourselves, Who am I to be brilliant, gorgeous, talented, fabulous? Actually, who are you not to be? You are a child of God. Your playing small does not serve the world. There is nothing enlightened about shrinking so that other people won't feel insecure around you. We are all meant to shine, as children do. And as we let our own light shine, we unconsciously give other people permission to do the same. As we are liberated from our own fear, our presence automatically liberates others. – **Marianne Williamson**

2. Optimism is the faith that leads to achievement. Nothing can be done without hope and confidence. – **Helen Keller**

3. The world steps aside for the man who knows where he is going. – **James Allen**

4. If you don't ask, the answer is always no. – **Nora Roberts**

5. I was always looking outside myself for strength and confidence but it comes from within. It is there all the time. – **Anna Freud**

6. Life shrinks or expands in proportion to one's courage. – **Anaïs Nin**

7. Believe in your infinite potential. Your only limitations are those you set upon yourself. – **Roy T. Bennett**

8. Don't say, "If I could, I would". Say, "If I can, I will". – **Jim Rohn**

9. Confidence is contagious. So is lack of confidence. – **Vince Lombardi**

10. You were not born a winner, and you were not born a loser. You are what you make yourself be. – **Lou Holtz**

11. Nothing builds self– esteem and self– confidence like accomplishment. **Thomas Carlyle**

12. Education breeds confidence. Confidence breeds hope. Hope breeds peace. – **Confucius**

13. You are the only person on earth who can use your

ability. – **Zig Ziglar**

14. Have confidence that if you have done a little thing well, you can do a bigger thing well too. – **David Storey**

15. Health is the greatest possession. Contentment is the greatest treasure. Confidence is the greatest friend. Non– being is the greatest joy. **Lao Tzu**

16. Happiness and confidence are the prettiest things you can wear. – **Taylor Swift**

17. A clear vision, backed by definite plans, gives you a tremendous feeling of confidence and personal power. – **Brian Tracy**

18. Don't wait until everything is just right. It will never be perfect. There will always be challenges, obstacles and less than perfect conditions. So what. Get started now. With each step you take, you will grow stronger and stronger, more and more skilled, more and more self– confident and more and more successful. – **Mark Victor Hansen**

19. If you haven't confidence in self, you are twice defeated in the race of life. With confidence, you have won even before you have started. – **Marcus Garvey**

20. The world belongs to those who set out to conquer

it armed with self confidence and good humor.
**Charles Dickens**

21. With realization of one's own potential and self–confidence in one's ability, one can build a better world. – **Dalai Lama**

22. You wouldn't worry so much about what others think of you if you realized how seldom they do. – **Eleanor Roosevelt**

23. Knock the 't' off the 'can't.' – **Samuel Johnson**

24. It's better to be a lion for a day than a sheep all your life. – **Elizabeth Kenny**

25. When you have confidence, you can have a lot of fun. And when you have fun, you can do amazing things. – **Joe Namath**

26. If you believe it will work out, you'll see opportunities. If you believe it won't you will see obstacles. – **Wayne Dyer**

27. Believing that the dots will connect down the road will give you the confidence to follow your heart. – **Steve Jobs**

28. You have within you right now, everything you need to deal with whatever the world can throw at you. – **Brian Tracy**

29. Put all excuses aside and remember this – you are capable. – **Zig Ziglar**

30. You gain strength, courage and confidence by every experience in which you really stop to look fear in the face. You are able to say to yourself, 'I have lived through this horror. I can take the next thing that comes along.' You must do the thing you think you cannot do. – **Eleanor Roosevelt**

31. I know who I am, I know what I believe, that's all I need to know. From there, you do what you need to do. – **Will Smith**

32. You cannot swim for new horizons until you have courage to lose sight of the shore. – **William Faulkner**

33. Action is a high road to self– confidence and self– esteem. **Bruce Lee**

34. Believing that you're enough is what gives you the courage to be authentic. – **Brené Brown**

35. Don't you dare, for one more second, surround yourself with people who are not aware of the greatness that you are. – **Jo Blackwell– Preston**

36. Believe and act as if it were impossible to fail. – **Charles F. Kettering**

37. Your dream doesn't have an expiration date. Take a deep breath and try again. – **K.T. Witten**

38. Don't live down to expectations. Go out there and do something remarkable. – **Wendy Wasserstein**

39. If you're presenting yourself with confidence, you can pull off pretty much anything.– **Katy Perry**

40. Be brave. Take risks. Nothing can substitute experience. – **Paulo Coelho**

41. Courage starts with showing up and letting ourselves be seen**. – Brené Brown**

42. My mother said to me, 'If you are a soldier, you will become a general. If you are a monk, you will become the Pope.' Instead, I was a painter, and became Picasso. – **Pablo Picasso**

43. There can be no friendship without confidence, and no confidence without integrity. – **Samuel Johnson**

44. Do not fear to be eccentric in opinion, for every opinion now accepted was once eccentric. – **Bertrand Russell**

45. Confidence and hard work is the best medicine to kill the disease called failure. It will make you successful person. – **Abdul Kalam**

46. There can be no failure to a man who has not lost his courage, his character, his self respect, or his self– confidence. He is still a King. – **Orison Swett Marden**

47. Confidence is preparation. Everything else is beyond your control. – **Richard Kline**

48. You can have anything you want, if you want it badly enough. – **Abraham Lincoln**

49. As is our confidence, so is our capacity. – **William Hazlitt**

50. Be courteous to all, but intimate with few, and let those few be well tried before you give them your confidence. – **George Washington**

51. A bold act requires a high degree of confidence. – **Robert Greene**

52. Confidence is going after Moby Dick in a rowboat and taking the tartar sauce with you. – **Zig Ziglar**

53. Man often becomes what he believes himself to be. – **Mahatma Gandhi**

54. The mind, ever the willing servant, will respond to boldness, for boldness, in effect, is a command to deliver mental resources. – **Norman Vincent Peale**

55. If one advances confidently in the direction of his dreams, and endeavors to live the life which he has imagined, he will meet with a success unexpected in common hours. – **Henry David Thoreau**

56. You have to expect things of yourself before you can do them. – **Michael Jordan**

57. Because one believes in oneself, one doesn't try to convince others. Because one is content with oneself, one doesn't need others' approval. Because one accepts oneself, the whole world accepts him or her. – **Lao Tzu**

58. You can be anything you want to be, do anything you set out to accomplish if you hold that desire with singleness of purpose. – **Abraham Lincoln**

59. Noble and great. Courageous and determined. Faithful and fearless. That is who you are and who you have always been. And understanding it can change your life, because this knowledge carries a confidence that cannot be duplicated any other way. – **Sheri L. Dew**

60. Confidence comes not from always being right but from not fearing to be wrong. – **Peter T. Mcintyre**

61. We have to learn to be our own best friends because we fall too easily into the trap of being our own

worst enemies. – **Roderick Thorp**

62. You have to expect things of yourself before you can do them. – **Michael Jordan**

63. Each time we face our fear, we gain strength, courage, and confidence in the doing.– **Theodore Roosevelt**

64. Life is not easy for any of us. But what of that? We must have perseverance and above all confidence in ourselves. We must believe that we are gifted for something, and that this thing, at whatever cost, must be attained. – **Marie Curie**

65. No one can make you feel inferior without your consent. – **Eleanor Roosevelt**

66. If you want to conquer fear, don't sit home and think about it. Go out and get busy. – **Dale Carnegie**

67. I am not afraid of storms for I am learning how to sail my ship. – **Louisa May Alcott**

68. "Don't be afraid of your fears. They're not there to scare you. They're there to let you know that something is worth it." – **C. JoyBell C.**

69. Life is not easy for any of us. But what of that? We must have perseverance and above all confidence in

ourselves. We must believe that we are gifted for something, and that this thing, at whatever cost, must be attained. – **Marie Curie**

70. Some people want it to happen, some wish it would happen, others make it happen. – **Michael Jordan**

71. Extraordinary people survive under the most terrible circumstances and they become more extraordinary because of it. – **Robertson Davies**

72. The secret is contained in a three– part formula I learned in the gym: self– confidence, a positive mental attitude, and honest hard work. – **Arnold Schwarzenegger**

73. If you don't have any confidence, you're not going to do anything." – **Stefon Diggs**

74. To be yourself in a world that is constantly trying to make you something else is the greatest accomplishment. – **Ralph Waldo Emerson**

75. For me, so far, confidence has been a journey, not a destination. – **Jessica Williams**

76. Somehow I can't believe that there are any heights that can't be scaled by a man who knows the secrets of making dreams come true. This special secret, it seems to me, can be summarized in four C s. They are curiosity, confidence, courage, and constancy,

and the greatest of all is confidence. When you believe in a thing, believe in it all the way, implicitly and unquestionable. **– Walt Disney**

77. Have confidence that if you have done a little thing well, you can do a bigger thing well too. **– David Storey**

78. My confidence comes from knowing I do the right things in my life. I do the right things in the gym. I do the right things all together. **– Daniel Cormier**

79. Anything is achievable. Be positive, be enthusiastic, and project confidence. **– Sarah Doukas**

80. The more you repeat to yourself that you can do it, the more that path will be grooved in your mind. **– Maxime Lagacé**

81. Confidence comes from hours and days and weeks and years of constant work and dedication. **– Roger Staubach**

82. The sun himself is weak when he first rises, and gathers strength and courage as the day gets on. **– Charles Dickens**

83. Anyone can give up; it is the easiest thing in the world to do. But to hold it together when everyone would expect you to fall apart, now that is true strength. **– Chris Bradford**

84. Everyone has talent. What is rare is the courage to follow the talent to the dark place where it leads. – **Erica Jong**

85. When you have a lot of confidence and you feel like nobody can beat you, it's game over for everyone else. – **Jason Day**

86. Take chances, make mistakes. That's how you grow. Pain nourishes your courage. You have to fail in order to practice being brave. – **Mary Tyler Moore**

87. You gain strength, courage, and confidence by every experience in which you really stop to look fear in the face. You are able to say to yourself, 'I lived through this horror. I can take the next thing that comes along.' – **Eleanor Roosevelt**

88. The most beautiful thing you can wear is confidence. – **Blake Lively**

89. Self– confidence is the first requisite to great undertakings. – **Samuel Johnson**

90. Get more confidence by doing things that excite and frighten you. – **Jessica Williams**

91. I've studied the lives of the 20th century's great businessmen and concluded self– confidence was

instrumental in all their success. – **Alex Spanos**

92. It takes a lot for you to find your confidence, but you shouldn't let someone else be the person to find it for you. – **Justine Skye**

93. Confidence. If you have it, you can make anything look good. – **Diane von Furstenberg**

94. If you have no confidence in self, you are twice defeated in the race of life. – **Marcus Garvey**

95. Confidence comes from knowing what you're doing. If you are prepared for something, you usually do it. If not, you usually fall flat on your face. – **Tom Landry**

96. I taught myself confidence. When I'd walk into a room and feel scared to death, I'd tell myself, 'I'm not afraid of anybody.' And people believed me. You've got to teach yourself to take over the world. – **Priyanka Chopra**

97. Confidence comes with maturity, being more accepting of yourself. – **Nicole Scherzinger**

98. Confidence is silent. Insecurities are loud. – **Joel Osteen**

99. Through my education, I didn't just develop skills, I didn't just develop the ability to learn but I

developed confidence. – **Michelle Obama**

100. With greater confidence in yourself and your abilities, you will set bigger goals, make bigger plans and commit yourself to achieving objectives that today you only dream about. – **Brian Tracy**

# CONTACT THE AUTHOR

Go to: https://www.facebook.com/fulfilling.dreams

Made in the USA
Coppell, TX
11 March 2021

51620663R00085